The Climate Change-Resilient Vegetable Garden

The Climate Change–Resilient Vegetable Garden

How to Grow Food in a Changing Climate

KIM STODDART

COOL
SPRINGS
PRESS

Quarto.com

© 2024 Quarto Publishing Group USA Inc.
Text © 2024 Green Rocket Group, LTD

First Published in 2024 by Cool Springs Press, an imprint of
The Quarto Group,
100 Cummings Center, Suite 265-D, Beverly, MA 01915, USA.
T (978) 282-9590 F (978) 283-2742

Cool Springs Press titles are also available at discount for retail,
wholesale, promotional, and bulk purchase. For details, contact
the Special Sales Manager by email at specialsales@quarto.com
or by mail at The Quarto Group, Attn: Special Sales Manager,
100 Cummings Center, Suite 265-D, Beverly, MA 01915, USA.

28 27 26 25 24   1 2 3 4 5

ISBN: 978-0-7603-8473-2

Digital edition published in 2024
eISBN: 978-0-7603-8474-9

Library of Congress Cataloging-in-Publication Data available

Design and Page Layout: Kelley Galbreath

Cover Illustration: Annie Davidson

Illustration: Annie Davidson, except Shutterstock on pages 1, 6,
7, 8, 13, 27, 43, 67, 81, 103, 121, 135, 153, and 183 and Mattie Wells
on page 60

Photography: All images courtesy of the author except:
Creuddyn: 18

Rachel Geddes: 14

Alberto Gentleman: 16 (right), 17 (right), 34 (bottom right), 102,
104, 187 (bottom), 192

Amanda Jackson: 132

Shutterstock: 5, 10 (bottom), 11, 19, 21 (left), 22, 25, 29, 30 (left),
44, 45, 46, 58, 60, 61, 62, 66, 71, 74 (right), 76, 85 (both), 86 (left),
96 (bottom), 97 (right), 120, 126 (middle, right), 129, 131, 140, 141,
147, 152, 164, 166, 168, 169, 170, 177 (bottom), 180 (both), 181
(right), 187 (top), 193 (right), 194 (middle), 196 (left, right)

John Williams: 9 (left), 12, 15 (top), 16 (left), 17 (left), 21 (right), 51
(left), 69, 70, 82 (bottom), 94, 134, 139 (right), 155 (left), 173 (left),
178, 184, 188 (bottom left), 195, 198, 204

Printed in China

Contents

Conclusion

How to connect with and enjoy your vegetable garden in a changing climate.

200

↑ Wasp on a leek flower head in my gardens

Introduction: What Climate Challenges Are We Facing, and What's to Come?

I'VE BEEN WRITING ABOUT CLIMATE CHANGE and gardening for publications such as *The Guardian* for more than a decade. When I first started, the on-the-ground reality of a heating, more volatile climate seemed far away or unreal for many. Sure, parts of the world were experiencing the long-predicted greater extremes of weather, but many places, such as the United States, United Kingdom, and Europe, simply were not—or at least not visibly so.

That's no longer the case. Now every area of the world is subject to extreme weather events, and they are becoming more and more frequent. According to the National Centers for Environmental Information, the United States alone has experienced more than 355 weather disasters since 1980, costing in excess of $2.54 trillion. The challenges are now undeniable and looming large.

The impact can be seen in our food production systems and on our mental health, and it is affecting our ability to garden and grow food as we used to. Changing seasons, coupled with much greater risk of drought, wildfires, storms, flooding, cold, snow, wind, and unpredictable rain, leave many of our traditional vegetable gardening practices looking vulnerable and exposed. There is also a greater risk of pest and disease as a result. All of this comes at a time when plants, gardens, and gardeners themselves may be left feeling weakened, damaged, and downright stressed.

With these topsy-turvy conditions, it is no longer gardening as usual . . . but this isn't necessarily a bad thing. For far too long gardening has been about work generation: about tools and tasks and exacting rules and instructions with a firm emphasis on keeping the natural world in check.

The Climate Change–Resilient Vegetable Garden looks to the past for inspiration for the future. It weaves in lots of savvy solutions, with an emphasis on optimism and easy ways to build resilience naturally: from robust soil vitality and plant selection to natural fuss- and product-free pest control systems. Plus, it offers lots of money- and timesaving

ideas that put people and the planet firmly center stage for a healthier, more biodiverse growing space.

If you are feeling frustrated, scared, angry, downhearted, and a bit helpless, it's totally understandable. This is why, alongside all the techniques, advice, and innovations outlined in this book, what I also wish to convey is a strong sense of hope: to let you know that there are solutions, there are opportunities, and there is hope, if we all work together within our communities and with others for the sake of the planet.

I also should mention that resilient, climate change–savvy gardening is as much about shoring up your own personal strength and abilities, as it is about the work you do on the ground in your growing space. Because of this, the book is meant to be a personal empowerment guide as much as a gardening guide.

So, let me take you on a journey into an altogether wilder, more free-spirited, rewarding, effective, and resilient approach to vegetable gardening. It puts food on your table, is environmentally robust, and creates an enjoyable, productive, and nurturing space in which to be—for the future and for us all.

You can do this. We can all make a difference, together. For person, plate, and planet.

—Kim

↑ **ABOVE, FROM LEFT**
Here I am in my own climate change gardens.

Boost biodiversity for greater resilience, naturally.

↑ I learned to make, save, mend, fix, and garden my way for free.

MY STORY OF RESILIENT GARDEN ADVENTURING—
FROM PROTECTED BACK GARDEN TO EXPOSED RURAL RETREAT

When I lived in the city of Brighton, in the southeast of England, I grew food in a small south-facing fenced garden. Vertical gardening and container growing were the order of the day. My move to the Wild West of Wales was in itself influenced by climate change. I had been reading a myriad of books such as James Lovelock's *The Revenge of Gaia*, John Seymour's *The Complete Book of Sufficiency*, and many others, and I was getting somewhat hot under the collar as a result. I was running PR companies at the time, and we were mainly working with ethical, eco brands and projects, but it was all about encouraging people to buy things to keep the economy moving. The more I read, the more I realized this was all, to a greater extent, highly flawed and vulnerable to the changes that were coming.

We weren't going to experience more pleasant weather with our changing climate; it was going to be about greater extremes of weather and greater risks—of flooding,

Why Working With Others Is Key

We in the Western world are in a privileged position compared to many countries that have taken a greater battering from climate change. Yet even at home, the impact of extreme weather events often is determined by class and economics. It is poverty that is the common denominator as money equals greater whatever-the-weather protection.

Being able to buy things is a privilege, and I think that the more we can connect and support our communities through our climate change gardening, the better that will be for us all. No matter your status or background, the planet is in trouble and we need to care for it. Growing food has the potential to be the greatest leveler; hands in the soil, plant by plant, person by person. In the process, hopefully we can take better care of each other and ride out this storm together.

→ Working together with others is key for the future.

drought, storms, rising sea levels, water shortages, more pests and disease—and the threats to food security that would surely follow.

It was going to shake the very fabric of our consumer-heavy existence to the core. We were living this featherbed-laden, soft existence, but there was a tsunami of change on the horizon.

I developed a secret, inner climate change–savvy wannabe gardener who longed to become hardier—to learn to repair, recycle, and renew, and ideally (I hoped) become part of the solution in my own small way. I'd sit in board meetings (bored) looking out the window daydreaming about what I could make out of pallets.

After I moved to my high-up homestead, I started on a resilient gardening mission. The process was documented initially in a series of gardening-for-free articles I wrote for *The Guardian* over the space of a few years. I wanted to see what was possible: How low-cost could food growing actually be? What could I make, salvage, and mend without spending any money at all?

For much of the time, I had to throw away the so-called rule book of gardening and experiment with old pre-consumerism knowledge and ways of doing things, mixed with the instinct and innovation that gradually blossomed as time went on. The more I did, the more my confidence grew. I learned many of the fundamental principles of resilience: they apply well to a more climate change–resilient vegetable garden, and the practices are gaining in popularity as awareness grows.

During my decade-plus of adventuring, I have experienced flooding (my vegetable garden was underwater for a few weeks), extreme drought that caused my private water supply to run almost completely dry (no water for the home, let alone the garden), extensive storms, and much more besides. So many of the techniques I cover in this book have been tried and tested in the most extreme of conditions.

Why Growing Food Matters

Nurturing some of your own homegrown, organic fruits and vegetables is a tremendously positive action in the face of climate change. In addition to saving money and putting food on the table, it reduces plastic and air miles. It also helps make you feel better and reduces climate change anxiety. There are resilient growing options available no matter where you live, and you can carbon capture, repurpose waste, and boost biodiversity in the process if you garden the climate change–savvy way.

↑ Earthy, homegrown happiness

1 How to Be a Resilient Grower

Why building resilience in the gardener is as important as building resilience in the garden itself. Plus, project ideas to gain confidence.

WE ARE LIVING THROUGH UNPRECEDENTED TIMES as the long-predicted greater extremes of weather create more challenging on-the-ground growing conditions. This, combined with the recent pandemic, the rising cost of living, and many ongoing threats, means that it's harder and harder to feel completely okay right now, let alone to make the necessary adaptions to your outside space to shore up the weather defenses.

It's no longer gardening, seasons, or indeed life, as usual.

This is why gardening in a climate change–savvy way is as much about connection and resilience in the gardener as it is the actual vegetable garden itself. It's about developing an innate, inner confidence and empowerment to think on your feet, to make decisions based around the weather at the given moment, and to break gardening rules if they require breaking. It's also about working with, and learning from, others, the individual growing conditions where you live, and the natural world at large.

We are all in this together.

Get Your Confidence Back to Help Build Resilience

Time and time again in the courses that I teach, I have gardeners of all levels putting themselves and their abilities down. They talk about their failures rather than their successes, even when they've gardened for a very long time.

← Building confidence and resilience in yourself (and your garden) is key.

↑ Here, I'm teaching climate change–savvy gardening at Kate Humble's permaculture garden and skills farm.

WHY IS THIS?

I believe that over the years, with our reliance on buying a lot of what we need and generally being told how we should (and shouldn't) garden, our confidence has dwindled in many ways. Certainly this is true when compared to our much hardier foremothers and fathers, who were able to grow food before there were multiple online purchasing options at our disposal twenty-four seven. Back then, there weren't so many tools, gadgets, and "must-have" items. There was no gold standard way of doing things. Tools were longer lasting because they had to be. People grew food in one form or another because they needed to eat. They were much simpler times in many ways.

Nowadays of course with globalization and modern technology so interweaved with the very fabric of our day-to-day existence, anyone interested in gardening is bombarded with images of the picture-perfect vegetable garden. On social media, online, on television, only the best side of gardens are shown. It's no wonder so many people feel that whatever they do is never quite good enough.

If you combine this false aesthetic with the overcomplication of the gardening process itself—more work to keep nature in check, and less time to work with it and play—then it's understandable. No wonder so many people feel like failures in light of the rather fake image that has been projected of what gardens should look and be like.

CHANGE IS IN THE AIR

Thankfully things are changing. The pandemic in all its awfulness and increasing climate change extremes of weather have widened interest in the natural world, the benefits of growing your own food, and connecting with wildlife in all its glory. People are seeking connection, money saving, and solace where they can through food gardening. These are green shoots of hope.

If we are to survive as a species and reverse the damage currently being unleashed on our planet and ourselves, getting in touch with the wonder of the natural world around us

A Climate Change–Savvy Mindset

Aim for a greater state of calm. Being in a greater state of calm (or emotional regulation) helps to stimulate the prefrontal cortex in your brain, which is where creative thinking, or executive functioning, comes from. In other words, this is the part of the brain that helps you to problem solve. If you are rushing around from job to job, feeling pressured to follow exacting lists or you are stressed, you are more in the "fight or flight" mode. This state will diminish your ability to think about what to do regarding our changing weather. It is essential therefore to create space to just be in your vegetable garden. Look, listen, and observe. Tune in to the wonder of the natural world. Let your worries subside and more creative ideas will start to flow on in.

Grow your confidence. Primped and polished gardens, focused on keeping nature in its place and every weed removed, often involve a lot of added fertilizer, work, and money—and they are not sustainable in any sense. These gardens are more expensive and time consuming, and they are more likely to be vulnerable to the elements. They also are unrealistic for the average Joe who just wants to grow some food and have a nice green space in which to hang.

Many gardeners feel guilty that their vegetable gardens don't look like those they see on TV or in magazines. Know that most of these are not maintained by one person, but by a team of gardeners, so it's unrealistic to create such a space on your own around the everyday demands of life. Be kind to yourself and others. Saving money and not being reliant on buying all your materials and plants builds confidence, skills, and feels very, very good.

Embrace the wild. A wilder, less structured garden can be as productive as a super-orderly one. Plus, it is much cheaper to run, is likely to be more resilient in a changing climate, and requires fewer time demands on you as its custodian.

↓ **BELOW, FROM TOP** I'm always looking for wildlife in my gardens. Every creature has its place in a biodiverse vegetable garden.

and the potential to nurture food into life, goes a long way. Tending a vegetable garden in a climate change–savvy manner is a tremendously positive step in the right direction, and one that has the potential to soothe, empower, and transform our lives forever.

WHY IT'S TIME TO BREAK THE RULES

Because it's no longer gardening as usual, we can no longer rely on the "gold standard recommendations" when it comes to gardening. The picture-perfect idyll I was just talking about is not real. It's not sustainable, and it's also highly vulnerable in the face of the increasing extremes of volatile weather we now face.

We need to break these rules of gardening when they don't make sense, and we need to build confidence in our abilities to make decisions based around the weather and what works best in our own outside growing space. Self-empowerment along with trial and error will be incredibly important to help us weather the storm ahead.

LOOKING TO THE PAST AND THE NATURAL WORLD FOR SOLUTIONS

If this all feels a bit daunting, then know that working with the natural world holds so many of the answers. What we know as the traditional gardening rule book is based on relatively recent "Manor House" practices of gardening, where everything was neat and tidy and under full control.

↓ **BELOW, FROM LEFT**
Don't be afraid of noninvasive weeds—they can be useful.

There are many seeds of hope for the future.

The future of vegetable gardening still looks bright if we ditch those formulaic instructions, which no longer fit the purpose, and tune in more to the natural resilience. It's time to let go once and for all of this false image of what a vegetable garden should be.

In the not-too-distant past, people saved seed from their crops, bartered and exchanged with others, made and mended tools, and built their own soil fertility. There were no soil pH testers, leaf blowers, synthetic fertilizers, or the like. People just worked with what they had thanks to the natural world and the materials nature made freely available to grow food to bring to the table.

It was cheaper, less time consuming, and much more robust than what we have been doing in recent times.

The Five Best Ways to Build Resilience As a Gardener

1. MAKE YOUR OWN COMPOST AND MULCHES

This is one of the easiest and best ways to tap into your inner resilient gardener. The pleasure of making compost for yourself out of waste materials from the garden, kitchen, and elsewhere is down-to-earth perfection. Easy to do in any-sized space with lots of different compost bin options, shapes, and sizes, it is a resilient gardener must.

↓ **BELOW, FROM LEFT** Leaf mold is a fantastic mulch, and it is free to make.

Adding comfrey to the compost pile helps it "cook" faster.

↑ Working by hand enables you to better protect and understand wildlife such as the newt I'm holding.

Likewise, mulches will help improve your soil and afford protection against greater extremes of weather (e.g., they help keep water in the ground for longer). They can be made out of locally sourced materials (also for free), and mulching can greatly reduce the amount of work required to keep plants suitably quenched. The timesaving and feel-good factors are guaranteed.

See page 73 for more on compost and mulch making.

2. STOP USING POWER TOOLS (AS MUCH AS POSSIBLE)

Power tools have been sold to us over the years as a timesaving, efficiency-boosting godsend, but are they really? First off, think about all the plastic and materials that have gone into making these items and their overall high energy consumption. On top of this, there are other issues with many of these fancy gizmos on the market. Know also that they don't make you a better gardener. Actually, overreliance can serve to make you a less connected, needier grower who is reliant on lots of stuff each year to grow fruit and vegetables.

Plus, with a shed full of machinery and gadgets you tend to look, touch, and feel your way a lot less than you would do otherwise. That can create a serious disconnect in your ability as custodian of your plot to see what is happening around you.

A lot of the time power tools are used to help keep nature firmly in check. Think, do I actually need to cut back or mow quite as much? Less is often more, resilience-wise. So, before you reach for the power tool as a default, why not have a look and think first about what is needed—and, perhaps more importantly, what is not. Nonmechanical hand tools, such as pruners, tend to provide you with more opportunities to feel your way and can provide a much better understanding of your plot and what is happening within.

Get Connected for More Intuitive Nature-Led Growing

Example 1: When pruning by hand I have seen that a dead branch is being used by a solitary bee, which are fantastic pollinators. I realized that leaving it in place over winter was a wise move. The last thing I wanted to do was destroy this bee's home.

Example 2: I let the grass grow long in various parts of my garden for biodiversity and flood protection (see page 48). I just mow pathways that enable me to walk about and access plants. Whenever I mow these pathways, or consider extending them a little, I do so slowly as you can guarantee I will see lots of butterflies, moths, and even frogs in the process. Treading carefully in the process enables me to avoid any damage to these precious and incredibly beneficial creatures.

3. MAKE, MEND, AND 'DO'

Rather than discarding something, think—can this be fixed or put to some other use instead? Whether it's cracked plastic planting trays secured with duct tape or loose raised beds nailed back into place, the process of problem solving and figuring out how to mend or repurpose a broken item will help you become more resilient for the future.

The so-called godfather of self-sufficiency in the United Kingdom, John Seymour, was (and still is) a massive inspiration to me. He recommended trying to produce little to no rubbish at all, to try to find a use for everything that you possibly can, to get creative, and to have fun in the process. I highly recommend giving it a go. The more you start, the more your confidence builds and the greater options for reinvention you will have at your command.

4. SAVE YOUR SEEDS

Saving some seed from your garden happens to be one of the best things you can do to create resilience. Although you wouldn't want to save seed from everything (and believe me I have tried), as this would be time consuming and all a bit much on a domestic scale, some seed saving is realistic and the rewards are many. Saving money is useful, but what's arguably more exciting is the knowledge that home-saved seed can become more adapted to your growing conditions.

Having been produced on your own plot, after a few years, the plants grown from seeds you saved will be better adjusted to your space. Think that's exciting? Well, then consider that in the process of saving seed, you also can select for the best traits you'd like to keep and make the seed even better overall. This could be choosing the best-flavored pea, or the bean plant that was the most productive, or the plant that did well despite a drought when all around it failed.

By choosing to breed and save seed from the plants that have fared the best, you can help ensure the seed you

↓ Saving the seed for greater climate change resilience for the future, together.

produce has these best qualities within. It's easy to do and a big step forward in sowing the seeds of natural resilience within yourself as much as your plot.

See page 103 for more information on seed saving.

5. FREE YOUR GARDEN AND YOUR MIND

A meticulously tidy garden is a lot of work and is likely to be more vulnerable to the elements. Working with the natural world more closely, by allowing wild areas, boosting biodiversity, and encouraging nature in to lend a helping hand, creates a less needy space. It also creates a plot that is alive and an extremely pleasurable and nurturing place in which to be.

Many gardening rules are no longer suitable, so try to ditch the exacting to-do lists and make time to question, think, and feel your way around what is needed to shore up the defenses in your vegetable garden. Get to know it better. Spend time just being there to think and let your natural instincts flow. Constantly rushing about will not allow time to problem solve or experiment with new ideas, which are absolutely key to a successful future.

Making your garden your own by really owning what works best for you and your plot is also important. Many of my best ideas have come from trying out new ways of doing things. Tune out the everyday noise of life and tune in to your inner resilient vegetable grower, and the ideas will come.

Nutritional Well-Being from the Ground Up

The quality of soil also affects the quality of our food. We all know that fruit and vegetables are good for us, and daily consumption of five to seven portions is an important part of a healthy diet. Yet, what happens if the produce we are eating is really low in vitamins and minerals? How is that going to have the same positive impact as food from a vegetable garden or field that is high in nutritional density?

It's simply not. All vegetables are not the same.

If you are eating produce that is lower in nutritional value, you have to munch more to get the same benefit as a smaller amount of higher vitamin- and mineral-loaded fare. Fruit and vegetables may well be delicious (and I know I'm speaking to the converted here), but it makes sense that we want to be growing and eating the best quality food there is. Quality is important; otherwise the quantity you'd need to eat to play nutritional catch up might turn mealtimes from a pleasure into an episode of Gardener versus Vegetables.

So how do we know the nutritional level of the produce we are buying or growing? There is increasing research into the greater nutritional benefit of crops grown with regenerative practices—in healthy, organic-matter-rich soil. In the United States, a 2022 study into soil health and nutrient density revealed some interesting findings that back this up. Specifically, the researchers found that crops grown on farms that practice a combination of "no-till, cover crops, and diverse rotations" demonstrated higher levels of certain minerals, vitamins, and phytochemicals, when compared to crops grown with conventional (a.k.a. synthetically fertilized and herbicide-treated fields).

It's just another example of the benefits of organic, homegrown food. By further enriching and protecting our soils with organic matter and boosting below ground resilience, we are in turn improving the nutritional quality of what we grow and harvest.

HOW TO NURTURE YOUR OWN INTERNAL BIODIVERSE GUT FLORA AND WHY YOU SHOULD

Soil health is important and there are clear benefits to soil that is alive with microbial activity for vitality and protection of the vegetables growing within. Let's now take a look at the human microbiome as it's interlinked with personal well-being and resilience in our changing climate. It is incredibly important that we look after ourselves as much as our gardens if we are to successfully ride out the storm clouds of the climatic changes rolling moodily on in.

Diet and Depression

There is much recent research suggesting fruit-, vegetable-, and whole-grain-rich diets can help improve depression symptoms. One study published in *Nature Communications* explored links between gut bacteria and depression. It was found that thirteen varieties of bad bacteria in particular seem to have a link with depression symptoms.

← **FROM LEFT** How good for you are the vegetables you eat?

Boost your soil and vegetable garden biodiversity, and you'll boost your own well-being with more time to enjoy your garden in the process.

HOW TO BE A RESILIENT GROWER

↑ Change is in the air.

There has been increasing interest in recent years in probiotic foods and all things healthy gut. This is because a healthy gut is believed to be linked to the robustness of the immune system itself. The idea being, the more in balance your microbiome (filled as it is with good and bad bacteria), the more strength and vitality you as a person are likely to have overall. Recent trials with fecal transplants intended to help patients with antibiotic resistance and fend off infection are just one example of studies being carried out in this emerging field.

Though it may seem like an emerging science, there's nothing new about it. Quite the opposite in fact. In the past, before the dominance of so much readily available packaged foods, every culture had some probiotic element within its diet. From raw unpasteurized cheeses, milk, and naturally fermented yogurts and breads in the West to delicious Asian pickles and sauces, such as kimchi and Lao padaek (fish sauce), there is a strong history of fermentation around the world. Possibly dating back as far as 6,000 BCE.

Yet with the rise of easily available processed food in the West and with concerns over the health and safety of unpasteurized milks, this ancient knowledge was sorely sidelined for many years. The dominance of sugar and salt-laden foods has been to the detriment of our health. Some people believe (myself firmly included) that probiotic foods are part of the solution to help ensure better human health for the future.

Arguably, equally important are the prebiotic foods that help feed the healthy gut bacteria the probiotic foods bring. It's all very well and good flooding your system with good bacteria, but it won't stay there unless you help enable it to flourish. It's a little akin to tending your own internal bacteria garden. There's no point planting out lots of good bacteria if you don't look after them. So prebiotic foods are important to microbiome resilience, too.

Here are just some of the best prebiotic heroes from the vegetable garden:

↓ Garlic is a fantastic food with so many reputed medicinal properties.

Garlic

This bulb has so many health benefits for the gardener (and the garden); it is a vegetable patch must. In my mixed planting system (more on this system on page 55), I pop these potent beauties in gaps in and around other produce wherever I can. There are many claims about the medicinal properties of this allium and the allicin within. Some people believe eating raw garlic in dressings, marinades, or sauces can help fend off colds. Yes, it has a strong aroma, but it is a vital prebiotic food, and the taste is delicious. If you are worried about the smell, just make sure everyone you are with enjoys their garlic, too. It is easily added finely chopped to salad dressings or on top of meals.

Leeks

These luscious vegetables also help to fuel gut health, so this is a good excuse if ever I heard one to get more of these hardy plants into your vegetable garden. Leeks can stay in the ground over winter to be

My Favorite Aioli Recipe

Homemade aioli is a great go-to garlic dip in my house. It's loved by kids and adults alike, and it's a good way of passing on the many bountiful benefits of this bulb. You may want to add more garlic to this recipe, so taste it and adjust it to your personal preference.

½ cup (115 g) mayonnaise, homemade
   or storebought
3 cloves garlic, peeled and finely chopped
   (or more, to taste)

¼ of a fresh lemon juice
Salt, to taste
1 tablespoon (15 ml) extra-virgin olive oil
Smoked Spanish paprika

Add the mayonnaise and garlic to a small bowl. Squeeze in the lemon juice, add the salt, and give it all a good stir. If you are happy with the consistency and flavor, add a drizzle of olive oil and stir it in. Sprinkle paprika over the top. This is best used fresh, but will store in the fridge overnight in an airtight container.

harvested when required. I also leave some in the garden to flower for the following year because the blooms are hugely ornamental and much loved by bees, hover flies, and butterflies. Who can blame them!

Asparagus

These delectable spears are so yummy to eat and so incredibly good for you at the same time. I have a patch in the polytunnel and a patch outside in my vegetable garden to try to maximize the length of the harvest season and the number of spears I can produce overall. If you've eaten asparagus before and noticed a slightly strange (hard to describe) odor change to your wee, know that this is because of the good impact it has on your insides. Grow as much and eat as much of it as you can. It shouldn't just be a luxury vegetable. Once established on your plot, these plants will keep producing for up to twenty years. It's an investment worth making.

See page 166 on perennial veggies for more on-the-ground growing advice for asparagus.

← Delicious Jerusalem artichoke—such a resilient plant, and so good for you!

Jerusalem Artichokes

These unusual but very tasty tubers often elicit knowing glances from gardeners who are in on the joke about their wind-inducing properties. It is true—they really are likely to make you pass gas. This side effect thankfully tends to dissipate the more you eat them as your body adjusts. Do also know that the reason they cause wind is due to their amazing probiotic nature, so if anyone asks, you are feeding your healthy gut bacteria!

More Prebiotic Additions to the Vegetable Patch

- Onions
- Chicory root
- Dandelion greens
- Apples have been observed to offer benefit to the gut microbiome also. An apple a day . . .

Make Your Own Ferments

Most people think of sauerkraut when it comes to fermented vegetables, and certainly the slightly sour smell of this distinctive probiotic food is a good measure of how other fermented food mixes should smell. Actually, you can work with most vegetables in this way by chopping, slicing, and grating your own delicious home-brewed, fermented concoctions.

2 Building Resilience from the Ground Up

How to nurture biodiversity below ground, and why it matters.

WHEN I MOVED TO MY HOME AND GARDENS in West Wales here in the United Kingdom more than a decade ago, I was faced with a third-of-an-acre vegetable garden with lots of weeds growing within. I did what was recommended widely at the time—I got a rototiller and turned the soil over. But it didn't feel right from the start. I watched in horror as everything in the rototiller's path was churned and destroyed. Soil structure, earthworms, and insects included.

And that was just what I could see. It felt wrong at the time, and as I began researching soil health and methods, such as no-till gardening, I watched as the newly turned over patch yet again became covered in weeds, more in fact than there had been previously. I later learned this is because weed seeds are resilient and can stay viable below ground for many, many years. They are brought to the surface when the ground is turned, rendering them able to spring into life with newfound gusto.

After just two uses of the rototiller, I stopped and sold it.

A few years later, when my neighbor's 10-acre (4-ha) sloped field behind my gardens was plowed in autumn, followed shortly after by a period of heavy rain, my vegetable patch became flooded. The soil in the field, previously held together by its covering of grass, had been robbed of its ability to retain water. Now newly turned over, its structure diminished, there was no holding back the flow. This enabled me to see firsthand the sheer vulnerability of dug-over loam.

When it was covered in grass, that field had been successfully processing a lot of rainwater for many years. I live in a very wet part of the United Kingdom. The root structure of the grass and the undisturbed soil beneath had a much greater capacity to hold water. Once this natural resilience had been removed by tilling it up, my gardens soon paid the consequences.

← My gardens have been designed with natural resilience and soil protection center stage.

Resilience Starts with the Soil

As this example demonstrates, and for so many other reasons, it's not just above ground we should be thinking of when it comes to building overall resilience. While below ground might not seem glamorous or exciting, it is increasingly apparent that many of the solutions to our current climate crisis lie beneath.

→ So much natural resilience lies below ground with the heroes of the healthy soil life.

Another Reason Why No-Dig (a.k.a. No-Till) Matters

The Netflix documentary *Kiss the Ground* brought to the wider public attention the idea that undug soil can capture and hold carbon. Whereas turned-over soil releases it into the atmosphere. Although the documentary mainly focused on the gain of carbon capture in commercial farming, the benefits of this approach to backyard and community growing could be huge. Your no-till vegetable garden can effectively act as a carbon sink and, when joined with that of millions of other home gardeners, can become a hugely important ally in the battle against global warming.

Every garden counts.

← Carbon capture and peat bog protection matters. Rannoch Moor peat bog in Scotland is pictured here.

In an organic gardening system, soil has long been considered center stage to productive, more nature-friendly growing: Chemicals and pesticides are obviously out. Compost and soil improvement are decidedly in. And the less we prod, poke, and till our soils, the better the natural world within can proliferate to our gain.

The soil below our plots should be positively alive and kicking, offering natural help and protection for plants and better resilience against rain and drought (see chapter 4 on water-saving techniques). We are just at the tip of the iceberg in our understanding of how microbial activity and fungi work in this underground domain. Their role is important and has been since the beginning of land life on Earth. Fungi effectively enabled plants to evolve and develop roots of their own over time. Still to this day the likes of mycorrhizal fungi bind themselves to certain plant roots to help them find food and water.

Below ground is an interconnected web full of hope, symbiotic relationships between microorganisms and plants, and potential for much greater resilience. Take trees growing

→ **FROM LEFT** Healthy soil is an important part of an interconnected, resilient world.

Healthy soil and healthy plants are forever linked.

in a forest—they can, through their roots and underground connectivity with fungi, sometimes come to the aid of a sickly neighboring tree.

With the increasingly challenging extremes of erratic weather, these networks of support can play a vital role in helping your plants and plots cope. It's therefore incredibly important to nurture soil health and natural resilience.

KIM'S TIPS

Viable Homemade Peat-Free Alternatives

Purpose	What to Use
Seed planting	Leaf mold. Also, wood chips that have rotted down for four years.
Container gardening	Homemade compost mixed with leaf mold
Boost fertility	Compost and manure
General soil amendment and mulching	Grass clippings, wood chips, leaf mold, loam, chopped comfrey

Let's Talk Water Retention in Growing Mixes

To replace peat, one key factor in the success of your mixes is its ability to hold and retain water. Leaf mold is a good addition as it works extremely well in this arena. Sheep wool is also very good, though it isn't widely available in many regions. Coir and wood also have good water-retention properties. If you can get your hands on some fleece, it can be cut up and mixed in the compost pile to pass these important benefits on. It also can be used as a soil protector and mulch over winter.

Materials Commonly Used in Peat-Free Mixes
- Bark, sawdust, chips, and waste wood
- Compost
- Seaweed and comfrey, for slow-release feed
- Coir/coconut-husk fiber

Coir is a waste material commonly used in growing mediums. It holds water and air. There are air miles associated with its use, so its credentials are mixed.

For a troubleshooting guide on using peat-free growing mixes successfully and how to overcome any common issues, see page 193.

↑ You want your compost to help retain soil water for healthy plants.

THE CLIMATE CHANGE–RESILIENT VEGETABLE GARDEN

Peat Free

There are so many issues with peat and so many reasons why its use is bad for our planet.

A garden cannot be resilient in the wider sense if it is using materials that cause damage to the natural environment. The mining of peat for horticultural uses since the mid-twentieth century has eroded the peat bogs and destroyed vital natural habitats. This has an impact on the wildlife that depends on these peat bogs, and the process of digging up these bogs, which are major carbon sinks, releases much CO_2 into the atmosphere. This further fuels the problems of global warming. This is why their protection is considered vital in the fight to save life as we know it on our troubled planet. Peat bogs have an additional role to play in the prevention of flooding, because they soak up and hold onto so much water.

Any way you look at it, peat use in horticulture is damaging. It's also not necessary, because there are an array of alternative materials with equally desirable water-retention properties that can be used in potting mixes.

Peat replacement is already happening in some countries. After much campaigning by many charities and groups, the government in the United Kingdom finally targeted the eradication of peat materials in horticulture use and products. It is now banned. Alternative peat-free mixes have been on sale in the United Kingdom for some time and, although there are still grumbles within the gardening community, most organic home growers are familiar with the available options.

In the United States, though, there is still a long way to go to become peat-free. Most of the peat used for North American horticulture comes from Canada, which contains an estimated 27 percent of the world's peatlands.

What will likely help with the global transition from peat-based growing mediums to peat-free mixes is the knowledge that some of the best substitute materials are actually entirely free. In fact, the use of peat in growing mediums is relative recent: It took off in the 1970s, and other materials, such as leaf mold, were used more widely by previous generations of gardeners.

We did it before, and we can do it again.

How to Boost Natural Life in Your Soil and Why You Should

In chapter 1 I explained the importance of the human microbiome. A good balance of healthy gut bacteria is believed to help boost our immune system, brain and mood functioning, and much more. Our soils are not that dissimilar. They also should be active ecosystems of microorganisms. From bacteria, nematodes, fungi, and protozoa to algae, arthropods, and many other organisms, when allowed to flourish, they work to the benefit of overall plant and garden health.

There is a symbiotic, supportive relationship that forms over time, the more you boost natural soil health and life. Microorganisms help feed plants by processing and releasing nutrients in the soil, they help maintain soil pH, boost water retention, and help build plant resilience against pests. Healthy soil really does equal healthy plants. And it's not just in one way. There is communication going on between plants and microorganisms all the time through the soil-wide fungal network. Soil really is alive. The plants provide this microscopic life below with little packets of carbohydrates produced through their roots. As leaves are shed and debris falls from the plant, it further provides valuable food to the life in the soil. It is amazing, full of wonder, and rich with resilience for all.

So why on earth would we not want to tap into this amazing potential within our soils?

The good news is that you can nurture soil life in many easy-to-employ ways. Think belowground biodiversity and you'll save yourselves oodles of time, money, and heartache in the process.

↑ Try to leave plant roots in the ground after harvesting, even with roots such as beetroot, whenever possible.

Employ No-Till (a.k.a. No-Dig)

If you disturb the soil, you disturb and damage this valuable web of life. See page 59 for more information on how to set up and maintain a no-till garden.

Reduce Fertilizer Use

If you feed plants synthetic fertilizers, they can get hooked on this quick-fix feed and can become rather "lazy" by not growing deep and strong roots that can acquire nutrition on their own. This can further stop them from forming beneficial relationships with the fungi in the soil. The result is shallower roots. Why should they bother reaching out when you are giving them all the nutrients they need out of a bottle?

Heavily fertilized plants need more of your attention and food as a result. They become less able to fend for themselves and arguably lose some of their potential for natural resilience. This, in turn, makes them more susceptible to greater extremes of weather because they have been coasting along being constantly fed. Slowly released, natural soil food is much better overall, because plants have to get off the proverbial couch and work harder to access the nutrients.

→ **CLOCKWISE, FROM TOP LEFT** A wood chip mulch protects soil over winter.

Wood chip mulching around a pear tree insulates the roots.

Working in tune with the natural world is key.

Protect soil and help attract wildlife below ground and above ground.

Avoid Bare Ground

Fallow ground is more vulnerable to the elements. The glare of the sun over summer exacerbates the risk of soil drying out and an excess of rain and cold can cause soil damage over winter. See page 41 on soil protection over winter for more advice on this topic, including how to use green manures.

Garden Organically

Chemical- and pesticide-free gardening helps this soil ecosystem flourish. It is essential for natural resilience. There has been lots of research looking into the levels of chemicals contained in vegetables that have been grown using pesticides, and the same concerns apply to soil. The chemical legacy lives on. The annual PAN UK report, which highlights that supermarket produce contains the most pesticides, is a truly sobering read. These products are damaging to soil life and should be avoided at all costs.

You, the gardener, have the choice to proceed in a more planet- and people-friendly manner. Thankfully, it's incredibly easy to do.

Feed and Nurture the Soil

In addition to feeding the soil with compost and using mulches for protection, you can create an attractive belowground habitat and that enables soil life to prosper to the benefit of your resilient vegetable garden. As much as we think of feeding aboveground wildlife, so should we consider the wildlife down below.

- **Try to leave plant roots in the ground** when you harvest crops. The roots you leave behind are food for soil life.

- **At the end of the harvesting season,** rather than clearing and removing all plant debris, allow some to break down naturally on the soil. It will serve as food for your resilience-boosting compadres below ground.

- **Biochar is also useful** (see sidebar on page 37 for more on biochar). There are lots of instructions online for making your own and many commercial options, often mixed with compost, now available to buy. This material helps provide an attractive underground habitat (and shelter) for microbial activity.

← Leaves as a natural mulch over winter can encourage microbial activity in soil.

BUILDING RESILIENCE FROM THE GROUND UP

→ Soil is good for
us as well.

TOUCH SOIL—IT'S SO GOOD FOR YOU!

Upset about something in your personal life?

Having a bad day and feeling stressed?

GO PLAY WITH SOIL!

Got a problem that needs solving?

Feeling overwhelmed with how much you need to get done in the garden?

SOIL IS GOOD FOR YOU, IT'S OFFICIAL

Emerging research suggests that touching soil is good for you. As well as helping you to switch off from the worries, chores, or stresses of the day, working with soil can make you feel good. This is because it stimulates the release of the natural antidepressant, or "happy hormone," serotonin into your brain. You need to be glove-free when gardening to tap into this mood-enhancing gain as it is the bacteria *Mycobacterium vaccae*, which provides this sense of well-being and it needs to be absorbed through your skin to work its magic.

Gardening in this close way also helps you to better connect with your vegetable plot and look and feel what is around. Doing so helps with the higher functioning decision making that is essential for problem solving. You can't think (or see) so clearly if you are charging about not looking closely.

The Benefits of Biochar

Biochar is best described as a form of activated charcoal. It is made from organic materials (such as wood, crop leftovers, or manure) through a process known as pyrolysis, meaning heating in a low-oxygen environment. It could tap into vast resources of agricultural and logging waste, turning them into a resilient soil improver for crops. It has huge potential. So much so that Al Gore talks about its "promise as an inexpensive and highly effective way to sequester carbon in soil" in his celebrated 2009 manifesto *Our Choice: A Plan to Solve the Climate Crisis*.

- **It can help increase microbial activity in the soil.** This is because it creates an attractive habitat, providing shelter for these microorganisms that helps them flourish.

- **Biochar can help improve the fertility of soil** and improve its structure and the aeration within. This boosts soil's ability to cope with water variations, enabling it to hold onto water for longer when rain is scarce and also helping to shore up the defenses against a lot of rain when the risk of soil erosion and nutrient leaching is high.

- **Because of the way biochar is made** (through the burning of organic materials without oxygen), the carbon binds to the biochar, which can then be used to feed plants and create carbon sinks safely in the ground.

- **One application is all that you need** in any one area, so this material's impact is lovely and long term.

→ Look, learn, and let natural systems in for super soil resilience and healthy plants.

How to Tell If Your Soil Is Healthy—a Quick Guide

LESS WORRY, MORE SOIL IMPROVEMENT

There are very exacting instructions with regard to what to do with different soil types, how to measure soil acidity (pH), etc. I'm not going to go there because I want to look at resilience overall and following these rules, regulations, and soil testing provides a distance that can be counterproductive. It can freeze the potential for natural instinct, connection, and ideas if you're fixated on the pH and other measurements of your soil.

I would use the analogy of trying to lose weight and standing on the scales twice a day to check if you are making progress. It can be totally disheartening to see any increase or slow progress. It's much better to step away, eat healthily, and exercise; then in a more relaxed way see from there how you feel and if your clothes fit. All the while ask yourself if the goals you have are realistic in the first place. Maybe see if you can reach the weight right for you instinctively and not through exacting measures. Everybody is different—what do you think you would like to be?

The same principles apply with soil—getting obsessed with your soil pH and other measurements can create barriers. It can create limiting beliefs: "My clay soil is so hard to work with. I wish I had sandier soil." or "I can't get my soil pH down, and I need to be *exactly* between 6 and 7 pH."

While there is no quick fix, adding lots of organic matter to the soil will improve its structure tremendously. Adding compost, going no-dig, and mulching go an incredibly long way. Try to worry less and use your energy to focus on working with what you have and improving your soil's structure naturally.

Telltale Signs of Soil That Is Healthy

- **Healthy soil** should look dark and crumbly.
- **Earthworm activity** is a good indicator of vitality.
- **Look for evidence** of a crumbly structure and fungi around plant roots.
- **Deep plant roots** that are well spread out also are good sign. They indicate plants are interacting well with the web of life below ground.
- **Most gardeners will have** the odd issue to deal with now and then, but if your produce is otherwise growing well with no overriding sign of disease or weakness, that is a good sign that your soil is healthy.

← **FROM LEFT** Healthy soil is alive with microbial and fungal networks and activity.

The prevalence of worms is a good indicator of soil health and vitality.

I harvest leaf mold to
use it throughout my
gardens.

Grass clippings
from mowing can be
used as a thin mulch
around plants.

Mulches, especially
over winter, are also
good for wildlife.

Lichen moving in
to help break down
the volcanic rock in
Lanzarote as it has
since the dawn of life
on land

Signs That Some Serious Soil Improvement Is Needed
- **Water collecting on the soil surface** can be a sign of compaction or drought-damage down below.
- **Pay close attention** if you pick up a handful of soil and it forms a sticky dense clump, looks pale, or seems devoid of life.
- **Check your soil** if plants seem to be forming shallow, stunted roots.
- **If produce isn't growing well,** leaves are yellowing or brown spotted, or plants are stunted it can be a sign of lack of fertility but also soil that is too alkaline.
- **If you have major issues with pests,** this also can be a sign of plant weakness through soil imbalances.
- **Moss growing on the soil** can be a sign of soil that's too acidic.

HOW YOUR ANNUAL SOIL CARE MIGHT LOOK

Please just use this as a general guide. Make it your own with what you find works best for you, your pocket, and your individual growing space.

Apply a Layer of Compost in Spring

This is to boost the fertility of your beds for the growing season ahead. Mix in some well-rotted animal manure if you have it. You don't need a lot (just a few inches will be fine) because you have your army of belowground helpers. Going no-dig and making this single application of food is all that healthy garden beds need.

Mulch during the Summer

This is especially useful around water-hungry plants. See page 73 for more information on how mulching helps reduce watering requirements and the ways to use different mulches, such as grass clippings, leaf mold, comfrey, wood chips, and more.

Another Mulch or Cover in Late Autumn

To avoid bare soil over winter, use green manures, mulches, and ground covers. There are lots of ways to keep all that hard-earned fertility in your soil, no matter the weather. See page 41 for advice on protecting soil over winter.

3   Climate Change-Friendly Garden Design Ideas

Tips to protect against the extremes, including the risk of wildfires.

← My climate change gardens have multilayered protection.

MY OWN CLIMATE CHANGE TRAINING GARDENS are in a very exposed location, more than 700 feet (213 m) above sea level. They have been subject to strong winds, flooding, and near complete drought as the water supply from my well runs drier each year. These conditions have enabled me to test out a lot of techniques in rather extreme conditions and to experiment with often simple-to-implement methods to boost all-weather results naturally.

Here are the most important considerations for vegetable garden adaptation and design, along with some further recommendations and savvy inspiration no matter which growing zone, country, or type of housing you live in. While the resilient design features outlined in this chapter will work for all gardens, I have included many that are useful for particular threats and challenges within our changing climate. Work to your risk, and experiment to see what is most useful and effective in your garden space.

Let Nature Be Your Guide

Before we get into the details and ideas of resilient design, and before you start putting them into practice, first thing's first:

↑ Tune out to tune in—you'll be awed by what you see!

Create space to listen to the sounds and sights of your vegetable garden. The rustling of leaves and garden birds chirping as they go about their everyday business, fluttering to and fro. Where do the birds live, and what are they feeding on? With no intention other than tuning in, just watch and let the awareness and ideas flow.

SWITCH OFF DEVICES AND SWITCH ON YOURSELF

All too often our phones accompany us into the vegetable garden. Try to switch yours off, or put it onto airplane mode if you can, to avoid the temptation to whip the phone out at the first sign of something exciting happening nature-wise. Don't get drawn into the noise of the daily news, social media chat, or suchlike. "A butterfly!" Snap . . . "A bumblebee!" Click . . . "What do I have to do this afternoon?" Email swipe.

We are so used to sharing on social media and being constantly connected online that it can feel a little strange to just observe in the here and now and just, well, be. It's all the more important that we train ourselves to spend some time without technology. Time in the garden should mean time without the phone.

KIM'S TIPS

Reasons to Be Mindful

- Mindfulness makes you feel good and reduces anxiety.
- Mindfulness helps create emotional regulation—a state of calm. Calmness is important for nurturing yourself, and it's harder than ever to find in our 24/7 world.
- In a state of calm, ideas flow. This is the creative problem-solving space. Climate change–savvy gardening solutions are found here.

It's just you and your garden and nature. That's worth its weight in gold.

↑ Create a naturalistic
rill as a barrier and fill
it with rainwater to
keep soil moist and
protect it against the
risk of wildfire.

Mitigating Wildfire Risks

Wildfires are an increasing risk in many previously unaffected areas of the world as periods of drought become more frequent. During a stretch of extreme and prolonged heat, plants, trees, and shrubs can themselves become a hazard (and indeed fuel) if positioned in the path of a wildfire. Because of this, it is important to afford protection to your plants and your home. Here are some ways to help with this.

FORM FIRE BARRIERS

Create a nonflammable barrier around your home and garden. Thirty feet (9 m) is the recommended fire defense zone to afford protection. Porous materials such as gravel, scattered paving, and stone are preferable as they also create a framework that can help you deal with an excess of rain. The water needs to be able to sink and flow away. Hard-standing surfaces such as concrete are great fire barriers, but they can cause issues with flooding.

Ideally you also want a nonflammable material zone around the outside of your garden as well as in between your garden and home, but this would use up a lot of valuable growing space in even the biggest garden, so innovative solutions need to be found. You want to be able to protect your plants and your home and still be able to have a thriving vegetable garden in the process.

→ Make a feature out of moveable planters and weave in some flowers for a biodiversity boost.

USE MOVEABLE PLANTERS

Smaller pots are easy enough to move by hand, but they have higher watering requirements (and less opportunity for natural resilience building). Bigger is always better when it comes to containers in the garden. You can source attractive containers on wheels that can be placed around your garden and moved if a risk of wildfire is imminent. You also can buy portable dollies that can be used to move growing gardens as and when required.

If you are using moveable containers in this way, consider creating using some paving stones within your gravel fire-barrier pathways. They will make it easier to move containers.

WORK WITH WATER

I don't think any garden is complete without a water feature or two. The sound of flowing water is incredibly soothing and nurturing. Inground water features will also come to your aid because dry ground is your enemy in a wildfire scenario.

Use Rills

These water pathways can be used to channel water to where it is needed if a wildfire strikes. In fire-prone areas, rills can be used as an attractive fire defense zone feature around the property and in the garden itself. They could then be fed with flowing water from a pond, rainwater collection system, or even the tap if and when required to provide a liquid barrier. See page 48 for more information on rainwater collection.

Use Ponds

Likewise, you can get creative with pond design around a central vegetable garden or near your home to create an attractive-yet-protective feature that will boost biodiversity as it helps to guard your home.

Use Drip Irrigation Systems for Your Boundary

Drip irrigation systems are useful for your resilient vegetable garden anyway and can easily be picked up and used around your property's boundary to wet the ground if your lot is threatened by a wildfire.

USE YOUR SPACE WISELY

Think "protection zones" when designing your garden. A vegetable garden in the ground needs to be protected, but your home also needs to be protected, too. The space between the two can be utilized with pots and moveable containers for most of the time with more defenses added as required.

SOIL HEALTH

This is always important for the health of plants, of course, but in the case of wildfire risk, healthy soil will help keep all-important water in the ground for longer, helping plants during a period of drought. Dead plants create a fire risk, so healthy soil is key to reducing that risk. See chapter 2 for more information on resilient soil care.

WATCH OUT FOR POTENTIALLY FLAMMABLE AREAS

A too-dry compost pile can ignite, so try to keep yours dampened down in times of extreme heat and drought. The decomposition process within can create a lot of heat, so also consider smaller barrel composting chambers to help minimize risk.

Likewise, a pile of dry branches or foliage can go up like tinder. Dampen any potential hazards to avoid being the source of a wildfire in your neighborhood.

↑ My gardens flooded recently, so I created lots of ways to slow it, spread it, and sink it, including a swale at the rear to help divert and soak up excess water.

Mitigating Flood Risks

Think slow it, spread it, sink it. Water will always try to find the path of least resistance. Because of this, your system of defense should be based around the central permaculture principle of "slow it, spread it, sink it." How that can look on the ground includes the following resilience-boosting methods, which will enable your garden to process much more water than it would be able to handle otherwise.

GET YOUR NEIGHBORS INVOLVED—COMMUNITY ACTION AFFORDS GREATER RESILIENCE

While there are lots of things you can do to help with your individual garden, in a neighborhood the actions of others will have a direct impact on the threat of flood. Because of this, it's important to work collaboratively to help shore up the community's defenses for the benefit of all. We are all in this together.

Rainwater Harvesting During Heavy Rain

If many neighbors collect water in their outside space, it will help stem the buildup of rainwater runoff. A single open trash can or bucket placed outside can help. An even more effective option would be rainwater collection systems in every home with a barrel or two per house to further reduce buildup of potential floodwater flow. The collected water can then be used to irrigate the garden, or at the very least, released when the risk of flooding has passed.

USE PERMEABLE MATERIALS

The trouble with hard surface areas, such as concrete and asphalt, is they don't allow water to percolate away. This causes issues because it means that water movement can then build up and up, to untamed levels that can cause flood risk as street drains struggle to cope with the large excess of water.

Consider instead permeable design with materials that enable water to readily drain, sink, or flow away.

- **Gravel**—cheap to buy and local. There are also recycled options available (repurposed materials from the construction industry). Use with a porous membrane beneath.

- **Permeable paving**—paving can still be used as long as there is some ability for water to flow through and away. Using permeable surfaces in your garden's design is very helpful, whether this is by placing gravel between paving slabs (you can buy resins that will hold the gravel together but are still porous); through the use of correctly laid brick pavers; or through the creation of gravel rills.

INCREASE PERENNIAL PLANTING

From trees, hedges, and shrubs to no-dig gardening practices, the presence of more plants in your community is rich with opportunity for long-term solutions (see page 52 for more information about varieties of trees and shrubs to consider). They will help the

↓ Further natural hedging, trees, and shrubs slow the flow of water and wind.

soil in your area handle an excess of rain much better than it would do otherwise. Robust, healthy soil with a better structure and lots of deep-rooted plants growing within can help soak up water more effectively and act as a valuable low-maintenance protection.

I have allowed some rushes to grow between trees in the forest garden I have planted on my homestead. This further helps with water absorption in an otherwise (at times) wet field.

WORK WITH WET AREAS

Rather than trying to fight nature all the time and control it, work with what you have. This is why wetlands exist naturally to act as a protective habitat that prevents flooding further down the line. If an area in your community is prone to being soggy, why not create a wildlife pond there with a rain garden and water-friendly plants growing around. A pond will be useful as an ally during periods of heat. It's an available source of water you can harvest for use on plants, and it will help attract beneficial predators to boost natural pest control within your growing space and that of your neighbors.

SWALES AND BIOSWALES

These manmade depressions or channels in the earth have been used around the world in flood-prone areas for a long time because they act as a useful first line of flood defense alongside other measures. I have a bioswale at the back of my training gardens,

The Wonder of Wetlands

Half the wetlands in Europe, the continental United States, and China have been destroyed in the past 300 years, according to research by Etienne Fluet-Chouinard from Stanford University. In parts of Europe, it's an even higher percentage, with Ireland at 90 percent; Germany, Lithuania and Hungary at 80 percent; and the United Kingdom, Italy, and the Netherlands at 75 percent.

Wetlands provide a vital habitat for a range of creatures (up to 40 percent of the planet's species live in this type of environment), but they also have an important role in the defense against flooding. Plus, wetlands further purify water as it soaks down through them and into the water table.

which have severely flooded in the past. It helps to soak up water and channel it away from my garden and home. I use this bioswale alongside further perennial plantings of trees, shrubs, willow, and long grasses.

RAISED BEDS

Lifting the plant roots up out of harm's way via raised beds is also useful in managing excess rainwater, so this is a measure I have employed in my training gardens. I have created a network of repurposed wooden based raised beds. The porous gravel pathways surrounding the beds enable rainwater to sink away. They also mean the pathways can be walked on without risk of damage all year round.

Mitigating the Risk of Strong Winds

As with water, you want to slow the flow of strong winds as much as you can to reduce the damage risk. Wind can cause irreparable damage to plants, trees, and shrubs that you have growing, not to mention homes and other structures. These types of plantings also lower the temperature rather significantly. Solid fences are problematic as wind barriers because wind can bounce off full force. Try these options for reducing the strength of wind gusts.

↑ **ABOVE, FROM LEFT**
Here I am in front of my swale with lots of perennial plantings.

Raised beds lift plant roots out of harm's way if the soil at ground level gets flooded.

CLIMATE CHANGE–FRIENDLY GARDEN DESIGN IDEAS

KIM'S TIPS

Orcharding Against the Odds

I was told categorically by a number of people that I would not be able to grow fruit trees so high up in such an exposed spot on my homestead. This of course made me immediately want to defy the odds and give it a go. I researched different methods and ideas, and found that quick-growing damson (plum) trees could provide a solution to my quandary.

I planted a row of three damson trees down the westerly side of where I wanted to place my future forest garden. Then I planted a selection of varieties of apple and a few pears in the area beside it. It took a few years, but once the damsons had grown up and into their space, their foliage provided just the barrier needed to allow the apple and pear trees to flourish and be protected sufficiently from the worst of the winds.

I think this demonstrates that if there is a will, there is often a way.

→ I have an orchard against the odds. The rushes help soak up water between trees and damson trees protect the apples and pears.

NATURAL HEDGING

This is an effective first line of defense against wind. To maximize harvests from your vegetable garden while also reducing your wind damage risk, why not create an edible barrier with the likes of soft fruit bushes, crab apples, wild cherry trees, or any number of native shrubs and small trees? Place this natural hedging along the side of the garden from which heavy winds usually arrive.

NATURAL FENCING

Materials such as willow and hazel can be used to create resilient hedging or wind breaks within your garden. You also can make a wildlife hedge out of old branches and clippings from your garden.

CREATE A LAYERED EFFECT

Think layers within layers to afford further protection. For example, I employ a mix of layers of hedging, wildlife hedging, willow, soft fruit bushes, and trees to slow the flow. This is a great all-purpose wind protection for my vegetable garden and polytunnels, and it also works well to raise the temperature slightly on cooler days and provide cool, partial shade on very hot days.

MITIGATING DROUGHT RISK

What if there is a heatwave and ban or restriction on water use? Learning to deal with drought is so important that I've dedicated a whole chapter to the subject later in this book. I cover water-saving measures in great detail in chapter 4, so I won't cover it again here, except to say it's another threat and challenge we will have to face more frequently.

Climate-Savvy Ideas for Improving Resilience

START FREE-PLANTING

I spent years religiously following an exacting crop rotation plan. It used to make my head whirl remembering the order in which to plant. It felt restrictive. I knew the organic gardening reasoning behind the rotation of crops. Yet, I also realized that closely planting large groups or blocks of the same plant meant that they were, by their mono-nature, more vulnerable because it made it easy for pests and diseases to move and spread from leaf to leaf and plant to plant.

↓ Lots of layered mixed planting offers protection against pest and disease.

Since I had an experience with my tomatoes that I shall refer to as "blight-gate" (more on this in a bit), I have been almost entirely mixing up my planting and writing about my experiences widely. I'm delighted to say in the past few years this method has seriously started to catch on as interest in permaculture and nature-friendly vegetable gardening solutions have grown. It's easy, fun, effective, and looks great.

Although I discovered this approach by accident and by feeling my way and just doing what felt right, it turns out it's much more akin to how people used to grow a long time ago. I wager that once you've tried it, you'll never look back or block plant en masse again.

Free-Planting As an Alternative to Crop Rotation

Although crop rotation serves a valuable purpose in an organic gardening system, there is a much more free-spirited alternative. Sure, you don't want a buildup of pests and disease or nutrient drain, and that is what would happen if you just planted the same crop in the same place year after year. Yet, the exacting system of *planting this* followed by *that* in a specific order can make your head spin as you try to work out what should go where and in which order. Not to mention that there are different recommendations of rotation to add confusion to the mix. On my third-of-an-acre plot I used to find it very difficult to follow indeed.

The Main Benefits of Free (or Mixed) Planting

You'll have less issues with pests and disease. If you have a block of carrots planted together, you might as well have a sign up saying "carrot fly, come this way!" You are making it easy for the pesky carrot fly to find what it is looking for. Mixed planting makes

KIM'S TIPS

From Blight-Gate to Blight Under Control

My second year in on my plot, my neat row of tomatoes in one of the polytunnels succumbed to blight. Despite my efforts to stem the spread, the airborne disease moved swiftly and with ease from leaf to leaf and plant to plant until the whole tunnel smelled of the destruction of my tomato crop. This made me wonder. Why am I planting like this, in straight lines, with all the plants in a row with their leaves touching? It makes them susceptible, and it doesn't make sense. So, I started planting crops from the same family separately and interplanting other varieties around the outside. I did this in a very small way to start and just built it up over time as my confidence in this approach and positive results ensued.

I entirely mix up my plants now with but a few exceptions. I learned afterwards that this system of less regimented planting is also known as a *polyculture* and had been used widely by peasant gardeners of yore.

As well as seriously helping to keep blight in check, I found it aids natural pest control, boosts biodiversity, and also gives your fruit and vegetable growing a fun, foraging edge that is hard to beat.

Free-Planting versus Block-Planting Potatoes

I have run trials on mixed-planted beds with a few potato plants versus mono-planted areas growing only potatoes. I found that the free-planting makes a massive difference in the health of my plants. It stops the blight from spreading—as the few tips of leaves that are affected can be easily removed. Whereas the potatoes in the block-planted bed succumbed to blight and were ruined within a few short days.

Mixed planting is simply the ultimate in low-maintenance, resilient, and fuss-free but productive growing.

Here's How to Get Started with Mixed Plantings
- Allow roughly 4 feet (1.2 m) between plants of the same family so they have sufficient distance between them.

- You can still plant in rows and have symmetry in your planting; it's just that there is more opportunity to mix and match plants and to do so in a way that works for you.

- Use herbs, salad leaves (such as lettuce and arugula/rocket), and flowers (such as nasturtium and calendula) as fillers in gaps. They are very light on the soil.

- I also like legumes (peas and beans) planted next to brassica (e.g., cabbages, kales, etc.) because the nitrogen-fixing properties of the peas and beans work well with the brassicas. Over time it helps feed them.

Savvy Tip: Leave pea and bean roots in the ground after you've finished cropping. The roots will decompose and release their nitrogen into the soil for future plant use.

↑ Mixed plantings in my gardens offer so many benefits.

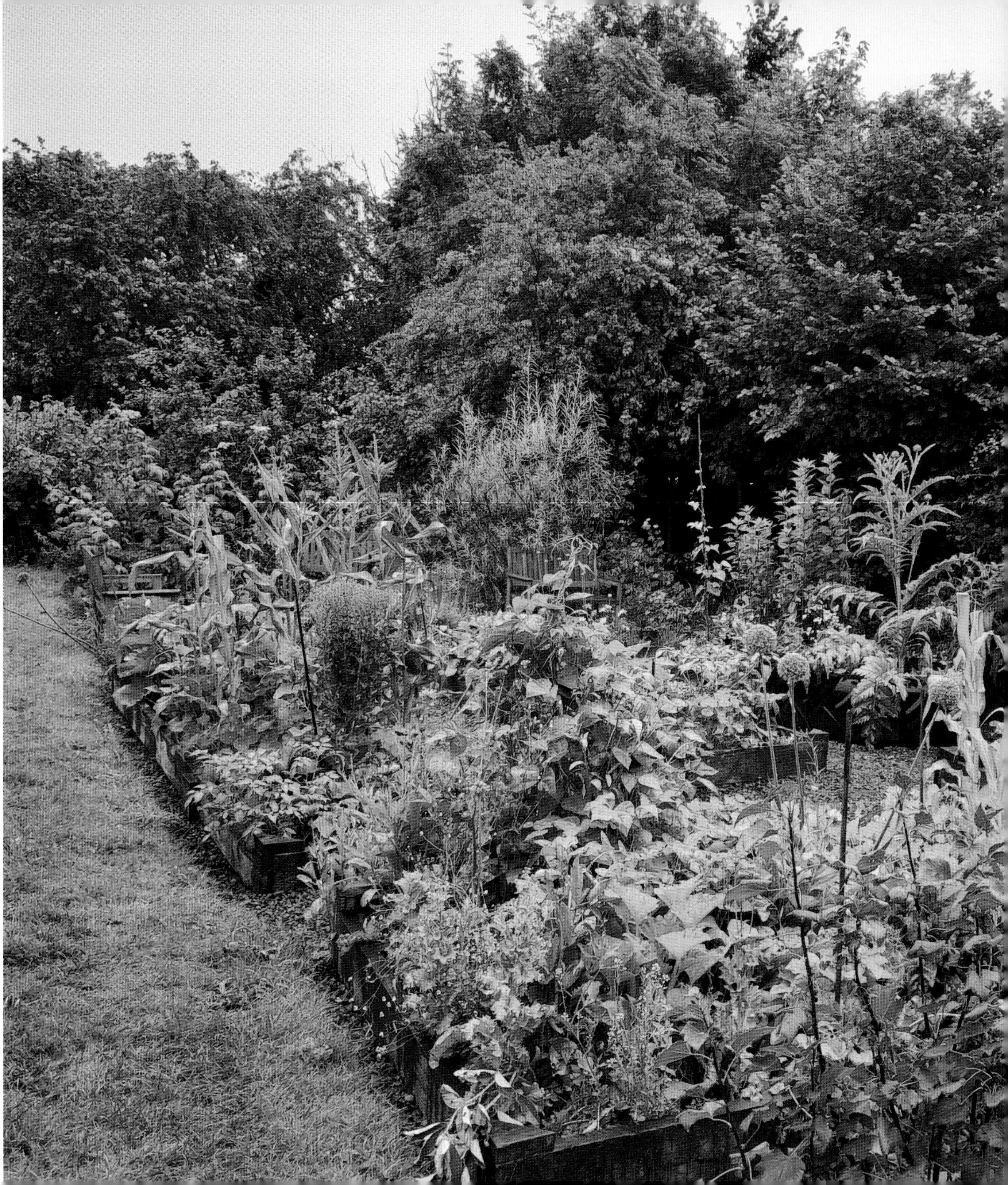

← Mixed planting makes it harder for pests to find what they are looking for.

it much harder for pests to proliferate as they have to work that much harder to find their chosen crop among all the other smells, layers, and colors of produce weaved in.

It takes less time and effort. This approach is lower maintenance because you are creating natural biodiversity on your plot. There is likely to be less watering required as you don't have all the water-hungry crops together in one place. Also, you will be using lots of crops as ground cover to protect the soil from drying out so quickly, and that means less watering for you.

It will hide your mistakes. Invariably something will not grow as well each season, and if you have an entire block of said something, then that really stands out. In a mixed planting system, when something hasn't worked quite as well, it will be hidden by other crops.

It is much more fun. I used to find that following exacting crop rotation systems becomes laborious. This way, it's more free-spirited and fun, enabling you to create a garden patch of your own design. I use lots of edible flowers as ground cover in between my crops for a splash of color that looks attractive and works for me. There is room to experiment here, and the process is enjoyable and empowering.

You can plant where you like. Because you aren't block-planting the same type of vegetable all together and therefore not enabling a buildup of pest and disease or a drain of nutrients from the soil, you can plant however you want to because you are mixing lots of different types of crops together. Throw out the rule book and have fun experimenting. It feels very, very good.

It is better for wildlife. Biodiversity will also get a boost in your garden as a result of mixed planting because it's much more akin to a natural ecosystem with many plants of different sizes, shapes, and heights all coexisting together. This creates a more attractive habit for beneficial wildlife than mono-planting alone, and it will help you create more a natural balance. The eat-and-be-eaten environment in your garden means lots of predators on hand to help your growing efforts naturally.

Think of it as companion planting just on a much bigger, more free-spirited (and effective) scale!

CREATE A NO-DIG/NO-TILL GARDEN FROM SCRATCH

There is this longstanding perception that starting a vegetable garden has to be expensive and that it has to involve lots of new equipment and materials. This is simply not the case, and an easy-to-build no-dig bed demonstrates this better than anything.

↓ No-till beds such as these are increasingly popular around the world.

THE CLIMATE CHANGE–RESILIENT VEGETABLE GARDEN

How to Build Your Low-Cost Bed in Just a Few Hours

1 **Think about where to site your bed.**
You can build it on grass or an area currently covered with weeds. If you build too near to wild areas or hedging, you might be drawing in an abundance of slugs—so give your garden some space around the edges. A sunny spot is preferable, and do think about all-important wheelbarrow access when making your decision. A level spot is also better to avoid soil loss when you water. Access to water is also an important consideration so you don't have to lug it too far.

2 **Quickly prep the area.**
If grass is long, give it a quick trim first. If you have lots of weeds growing on the site, it's worth doing the same. Use a lawn mower if you have one to cut them back; it makes it easier at the next stage.

3 **Get cardboard down.**
Cardboard is your permeable base layer. Just remove any staples and tape and place it down on the area you wish to transform into a bed. Overlap the edges and watch out for any gaps because weeds will use those to sneak on through.

If you have a lot of invasive weeds growing in this space, add a couple of layers of cardboard, instead of just one, to further hold them back. Yes, the cardboard will break down over time, but the idea is that it holds back the weeds and grass below and eventually it decomposes and becomes food for the soil life and plants in your vegetable garden.

4 **Build the structure.**
You can create temporary sides to your bed with planks of wood, stone, or slate. Use whatever you have on hand. Or you can create a fixed structure by securing these materials in place around and on top of the cardboard, ensuring there are no gaps.

5 **Add your growing medium.**
Give your cardboard bed a quick water first because this helps the compost you are about to add bind to it better. You need an initial layer of about 4 to 6 inches (10 to 15 cm) of growing medium. This can be compost mixed in with some topsoil, manure, or leaf mold that you have more readily at hand. On grass, a depth near 4 inches (10 cm) of material is fine, but it's a good idea to add a bit more if you have placed your new bed on top of weeds.

6 **Think about future pathways.**
You can extend your cardboard further out either side of your new bed to smother grass or weeds surrounding it. These can later become pathways if you'd like. (One thing at a time for now.)

7 **Time to get planting.**
And away you grow. There is enough growing medium to plant onto and the cardboard down below will start to break down after a few months to enable your seedlings to further access the lovely nutrients in the native soil below. Until then, if you're planting deeper-rooted plants that might prefer more underground space, give the cardboard a poke with a soil knife or a pair of pruners before planting out transplants so their roots are given a helping hand breaking through it.

That's it. You might find some weeds poking their way through in the first year, but they can simply be removed. The grass and whatever was growing below will break down with time and help provide nutrients for your new bed (and the soil life below it) for years to come.

→ A hügelkultur
bed design

THINK OUTSIDE THE BED

Hügelkultur

Often referred to as the ultimate in low-maintenance raised beds, once constructed, this mound (or hill) bed doesn't require any watering at all. It can be made out of leftover garden materials and planted almost from the word go. It is a centuries old method used most commonly in Germany and Eastern Europe, and it is well worth a look.

To make your hügelkultur bed, you'll need some logs or thick branches, homemade compost, leaf mold, grass clippings, wood chips, and plant debris. If you are using large logs, dig a trench and layer them on the bottom. Then cover the logs with some of your other materials to fill in, press down to avoid too many gaps, and then begin adding the other layers to create your mound. Any order is fine; you just want a layer of compost or topsoil to go on last to cover it over. This final layer should be about 5 inches (13 cm) deep or more to give your plants the best start.

You can then plant the likes of potatoes (as a good pioneer crop), squash, green-leafed brassicas (such as spinach or kale), alliums (such as onion and garlic), and lettuce in your first few years before branching out into growing other crops.

The decomposing woody materials at the bottom of the bed release nutrients as they break down, and the spongy materials within help the mound hold onto water—hence the reason why no irrigation is needed. Over time as the heap breaks down, you can widen the range of produce that can be planted in your bed.

Further idea—why not place your hügelkultur bed in your swale? It's a perfect spot to help further shore up the defenses against flooding. Does that make it a hügelswale? Call it what you prefer—just make it your own.

Free-Planting Outside the Box

As I've already outlined, there can be a much more free-spirited approach to planting that affords greater resilience. No lines or block-planting needed (at all). So why not then consider expanding this vegetable growing philosophy out into other growing areas? If you have a flower garden, orchard, or alternative garden beds, consider planting some produce in and around your trees, shrubs, or flowers. It's taking the idea of mixed planting to whole new levels.

Part forest garden, part polyculture, part doing what works for you—the results are delicious homegrown edibles to bring to the table.

Guerrilla Gardening in Your Community

Resilience is about you, your garden, and working with others, so why not look further afield and be community minded? From planting some edibles outside your front door for passersby to pick and enjoy to the making of "seed bombs" that use a mixture of compost and clay to house seed for wild plantings on bare patches of ground, expand your garden out far and wide as much as you can. You'll be maximizing positive impact and planting seeds of hope for the future.

↓ Think outside the traditional bed. Work with locally available materials to create your own style.

→ **FROM LEFT** Make your own little community capsules of hope (a.k.a. seed bombs).

My gravel herb garden produces as many fresh kitchen herbs as I can use.

Keyhole Gardening

This method of gardening is often used in countries where soil fertility is poor. It involves the creation of a bed around a compost bin. The idea being that the materials in the composting section will provide nutrients that feed the soil surrounding it to the benefit of the plants growing there. It invariably takes the shape of a keyhole, hence the name.

There is also trench gardening. This method involves burying compostable materials directly into the soil, covering it over, and planting right into it.

Gravel Garden

Gravel is a truly amazing material, and it's not just for pathways. It can be used to create beds for growing in. Gravel creates the perfect low-maintenance, permanent mulch, holding water in the soil beneath. Although most commonly associated with Mediterranean-style plantings of ornamentals (such as the Beth Chatto Gardens in the United Kingdom) and dry gardening, it also can be used for certain perennial edibles.

I have lots of herbs growing in a gravel rockery area by my polytunnels. The chives, mint, rosemary, and other herbs I have growing there thrive, unwatered by me. They also help draw pollinators and beneficial creatures into my growing areas.

To create a gravel herb garden, cover your chosen area with a porous membrane and weigh the sides down with rocks to create an edging. Then make holes where you would like your plants to go and fill these holes with compost before adding your herbs. Add your gravel in and around the plants. I also used field stones and slate in the areas between to create a further feature.

This technique keeps super resilient herbs, such as mint and chives, contained, watered, and fed with no further input required.

Lasagna Beds

This low-cost option involves layering organic materials such as grass clippings, wood chips, and leaf mold into a makeshift bed. Add a layer of cardboard first if there is grass or weeds present. Finish with some compost on top, and you can plant straight into your layered bed right after constructing it.

Further Gravel Ideas

I have experimented with growing raspberry canes in gravel. It helps reel in their spreading tendencies and reduces watering needs. I also have been interested to see time and time again how strawberries runners seem to like growing in gravel and how much they prosper in gravel pathways. At first I thought they must have somehow sent their roots through the porous membrane beneath the gravel to access the soil beneath, but upon inspection they hadn't. They were rooted only in the gravel.

I've also had lettuce, chives, and other self-seeding edibles just randomly grow in gravel. Because of this, I was interested to read about emerging research into the potential for growing in aggregates such as gravel, including how the minerals from the stone itself can help feed plants with the addition of water.

This is an area of gardening I am playing with now to see how much I can grow.

↑ Strawberry plants flourishing in just gravel

Never Stop Experimenting

This is key. There are always new ideas and ways of doing things, and the more we can be open, the better prepared we will be and the more fun we can have in the process of building resilience—both into our outside spaces and within ourselves.

WEAVE IN THE WILD

The greater variety of plants you can have in your gardens, the more opportunity there will be for wildlife to proliferate. This is why noninvasive weeds have an important role to play. Although you don't want them taking over, the creation of wilder planting areas should be considered a priority. It could just be in a few corners or one dedicated area, but it all makes a value contribution to boosting that all-important biodiversity.

Certainly in the case of bees, having plants that flower as much of the year as possible, and at different times, is incredibly useful. Dandelions, for example, are a fantastic and important source of food for pollinators early in the season when little else is available.

Obviously Organic

Multifarious weed killer and pest-destroyer products we now see adorning garden center shelves are only a relatively recent invention, all things considered. In the past, before gardening and farming became so commercialized, people grew crops in tune with the natural world without such products.

In a balanced and biodiverse space, such products are simply not needed. In many cases, these quick-fix interventions will create more damage and vulnerability on your plot. They have no place at all in a climate change–savvy garden.

There's nothing new about organic. It's the way things used to be done. It's the way we need to be moving forward, for the sake of us all.

4 Saving Resources

How to reduce water use by capturing rainwater, layering plants, mulching properly, and irrigating in a more regenerative way.

AS OUR PLANET WARMS, droughts and heatwaves are becoming more and more common. Concurrently, we are seeing increasing water-use restrictions and bans thanks to shortages of water as infrastructures and authorities struggle to keep up with demand.

It's no longer gardening as usual and that means it's no longer watering as usual.

Knowing how to look after your plants effectively during a period of drought is essential. Being informed about how to make the best use of this precious resource and make what water you do have go further also is incredibly important. Because we've become so reliant on turning to the online gardening store for everything we need and treating vegetable growing as a high-demand product and instruction-laden enterprise, our watering practices have become somewhat time and water heavy. Primped and polished gardens simply need more liquid refreshment. By keeping nature more firmly in check, an outside space becomes more vulnerable to the elements and increasingly needy.

We need to start thinking differently about water and the way that we use it. By working more regeneratively in the design and care of our vegetable gardens, and by working with the right produce for our place, we can create more robust plants that are better able to fend for themselves. In turn, they will have fewer exacting watering needs and will be better able to stand firm, no matter the weather.

This is certainly better for the gardener with less to and fro, laborious watering requirements that, let's face it, can become stressful even when water is in ample supply. It is better for the plants themselves, too, because too much watering makes them more

← Rain matters—it's a precious resource we all need.

↑ This wildlife pond/ rain garden is being fed from rain barrels and a rill to collect rainwater, making a great place for frogs and other wildlife.

needy of our attention and more vulnerable. And lastly, it's better for the planet because we are making better use of this precious, diminishing resource.

For person, plate, and planet, here's how to get truly waterwise by working with the natural world to reduce your consumption and boost natural resilience overall.

Why Water Is an Issue

Water is at the heart of the challenges we are facing and will face in our changing climate, from rising sea levels and flooding to an increasing risk of drought and water shortages. According to an October 2022 report by the Intergovernmental Panel on Climate Change (IPCC), roughly half the world's population is experiencing what could be termed as severe water scarcity for at least part of the year. These numbers are only going to increase as our planet warms.

Extreme Experience— Gardening with Very Little Summer Water

My homestead relies on a private water supply (a well), and for the last few years, the supply has been dipping more and more each summer, running almost entirely dry for months at a time with a mere ten gallons a day coming in, which isn't enough to supply a home, let alone a garden. A summer water-use ban would be a good comparison to so little water being available on tap.

Yet, this experience has been incredibly useful because it has enabled me to further test the techniques I use to a whole new level of dryness. For a few summers running, I hardly watered the plants in the ground in my polytunnels, vegetable garden, and large raised beds for weeks on end during a drought and was amazed at how well the majority of my plants fared. Seedlings in small pots were watered because they are much more vulnerable, but the vegetables in the ground had to tough it out.

There are many reasons why they did so well. Healthy, robust soil with natural ecosystems supporting plants from below, my free-planting system, and use of ground cover to protect soil from the sun are a few of those reasons. Also, I let plants trail and grow wild to further afford natural protection. And when I did water, I ensured it went deep into the soil and I mulched well. The trailing plants also became a natural mulch in themselves.

Although I'm not suggesting you need to water quite so little as I did, I offer this example to show how resilient plants and gardens can be, to show that it is going to be okay. There are solutions—and low-maintenance ones at that.

Climate change–savvy gardening also is very much about adaptation to the challenges at hand. In my case, I have further widened my rainwater capturing systems as a result. You can never have too many vessels for water capture. I am also backing up the private water supply for the home with alternative supplies to keep us from running quite so low again. There's nothing like turning on the tap and finding it's completely dry to bring the reality of our changing climate robustly to the forefront of your mind.

↓ In one of my polytunnels, I'm still smiling as plants are flourishing despite my well running almost dry.

The World Economic Forum states water scarcity is a critical concern on the sustainability agenda. Only 1 percent of the Earth's surface is accessible drinking water. Water-use restrictions and food security concerns will only increase as supplies further dwindle, making home and community grown crops more important than ever. Learning how to grow with reduced water input is absolutely key. It is further essential to harvest and store this precious resource when it is in ample supply to help reduce pressure on main supplies when they are challenged.

How to Water Wisely

First things first, let's look at how to make the best use of the water you have when it comes time to water your plants. Then, we'll ease into other ways to reduce water consumption.

WHEN TO WATER

Water applied during the heat of the day is much more likely to be wasted because it quickly evaporates. Liquid refreshment early in the morning or much later in the day when temperatures are cooler enables the water to permeate deeper into the ground where the plants need it most.

↓ Make your water count.

How to Water—Deeply and Less Often

It's important to water the soil itself, not your plant's foliage. Any moisture that lands from above onto plant leaves is more likely to be wasted. What you want is proper deep watering so the liquid can travel down into the ground where its benefit can last for much longer. A quick surface watering will dry off quickly, and its impact will be short term.

On the opposite spectrum, too much watering can make plants a bit lazy and prevent them from forming beneficial relationships with organisms such as fungi below the ground that help them source food and water. They also can form a shallower root system as a result, so don't pamper them too much. They'll only become spoiled and needy if you do. A bit of tough love goes a long way toward nurturing more natural resilience.

Other Irrigation Inspiration Can Be Sought from Around the World

On the island of Lanzarote in the Canary Islands, which are dry and the soil volcanic, small half-circle walls are built out of rock to provide shelter and capture condensation from the fog. A grape vine or another crop is grown within each. You may also see plastic bottles on sticks positioned by crops for the same reason, to provide a slow-drip release of water captured through condensation.

In other places, untreated, porous clay pots are buried in the ground to supply crops in dry climate with water as they need it (when the soil surrounding is dry). This technique has been used around the world since ancient times.

← Resilient fog condensation-capturing stone gardens in Lanzarote, the Canary Islands

What Watering Systems to Use

- **Overhead sprinklers:** These water the foliage of the plants as much as the soil, and some of that liquid will be wasted.

- **Ground-level drip systems:** These provide a regular supply deep into the soil where it is needed most, but it tends to be small amounts at any one time so some of the liquid can dry off before it soaks in.

- **Handheld hose spray:** This can be used to water soil deeply all in one go, so it is my preferred option. Although it takes time to do, I don't have to do it that often because I am watering deeply for much longer. I also can attach the hose to my rainwater harvesting systems.

- **Handheld watering can:** This has its place, too, although it requires a lot more back and forth with filling. I use this for some of my rainwater harvesting supplies that are harder to reach.

HOW TO CREATE A GARDEN THAT IS LESS NEEDY FOR WATER IN THE FIRST PLACE

Create a Healthy Soil Ecosystem

As outlined in chapter 2, it's important to boost nature resilience below ground as this will enable your soil to hold and maintain more water than it would do otherwise. With greater structure, life, and vitality, natural systems of support can come into play, reducing the amount of water you need to provide. It's no-dig, organic simplicity at its best with an array of microorganisms to lend a helping hand.

↓ Crops such as winter squash and pumpkin have sprawling leaves that can protect the ground from drying.

Savvy Tip: Avoid disturbing the soil when harvesting crops. Where possible, cut the crop off at the stem, leaving roots in the ground. You also can use some of the cut plant leaves as an impromptu mulch—it will further feed and protect the soil and the abundant life within.

Keep Soil Protected with Ground Cover

Bare soil is much more vulnerable to the drying glare of the sun during a hot spell. Exposed soil will dry out a lot quicker than soil that is covered with plantings. Growing more edibles, more often, makes the best use of your space productivity-wise, and filling your beds with mixed plants will help keep soil underneath moist for longer periods of time.

Layered, free-planting helps exceptionally well in this regard as it provides shade and a greater diversity of plants with different watering requirements overall. Fill any gaps in your beds with quick-growing crops, such as salad leaves, nasturtium, and calendula, and use the sprawling leaves of plants to create shade. Let the likes of squash and pumpkin trail around other crops to afford protection.

Also consider letting some of your fruits grow wild and trail along the ground in a heatwave. This is a technique I have used successfully to help plants cope when my well has run near dry. Tomatoes and cucumbers were allowed to trail along beds and over the sides into my gravel pathways. They showed no sign of blight in my mixed planting system and this way they were able to further seek out water through additional rooting points along their stems.

I was inspired to do this by the wild tomatoes I have seen growing on roadsides in many Mediterranean countries. Tomatoes especially will readily root via their stems if they are placed in contact with soil.

Use Mulches

After a good, deep watering, mulch will help keep water in the ground underneath for longer, so it's incredibly useful. It will further feed the soil and build structure as it breaks down. Many freely available materials can be easily used for this purpose, so it is a climate change garden must.

↑ **ABOVE, FROM TOP** Use ground-covering plants such as nasturtium to help keep water in.

During a drought I let my tomatoes grow wild and trail. This enables the stems to root as they grow and manage with hardly any water at all.

You only need a thin sprinkling of a few inches/centimeters, and you can choose from any of the following that you have at hand.

- Wood chips
- Leaf mold
- Comfrey leaves, chopped or torn
- Compost
- Grass clippings
- Spent plant foliage laid down on the ground

Work with Perennials and Drought-Tolerant Plants
Their deeper-rooted, longer-lived nature enables perennials to seek out food and water from a much wider area. In a healthy soil system, they also are much more likely to have formed attachments to the mycorrhizal fungi in the soil, which will come to their aid during

↓ **BELOW, FROM LEFT**
Ground cover and trailing crops afford protection for your soil by keeping water in.

This permaculture herb spiral has lots of ground-covering plants to keep moisture in.

times of water scarcity. Try to weave in as many perennial crops as you can. It's less work for you and will result in more low-maintenance, resilient edibles year after year, whatever the weather.

There is more information on recommended varieties and planting options in chapter 9 in the vegetable planting guide.

Savvy Tip: Saving seed from produce that shows extra resilience in the face of drought is incredibly beneficial. These are traits you seriously want to encourage in your home-saved seed supply.

Create Layered Protection

Some shade can really help gardens and gardeners deal with a prolonged period of heat. Providing some shade means that plants are getting the benefit of the sun and also being afforded some protection from its powerful glare when the thermostat is high.

Use taller plants and structures to create some respite for surrounding plants. Position plants that are likely to find the heat more challenging in positions of greater protection to help them cope. Free-planting helps in this regard, and each bed will be a layer of different sized and structured planting.

In particular, Jerusalem artichokes (see page 169) are an ally as they can be grown on the outside of a vegetable garden to provide some shade. They are super-resilient perennial edibles.

Leave Plants in the Ground for Longer

Push back on the idea that plants have to be whipped out of the ground as soon as they have mainly finished producing. Many vegetable plants will keep producing for longer if you'll just give them half the chance. This works well for soil protection and also makes the best use of what you have for further harvests. For example, lettuce, arugula/rocket, summer herbs, and peas and beans can often be cut back to encourage further production.

A Word on Lawn Care

Grassed areas can be very vulnerable to periods of drought—short, manicured lawns especially so. How well our lawns will fare in the future is questionable, but certainly longer grass with some wild plants growing within will cope a lot better. Such areas also act as beneficial habitats for pollinators and help boost biodiversity.

↑ Spot the difference: a summer lawn before and after a cut. You can see clearly which looks healthier.

↑ Water barrels at
the ready!

RAINWATER HARVESTING GUIDE

While we are scrambling around trying to reduce water use and protect our plants during the summer, the flip side of the climate change coin is that an excess of water and flooding are prevalent. From one extreme to the other we flip, so let's make use of this resource when it is in ample supply (it will help reduce flooding risk to harvest rainwater, too).

Any size property with some outside space has the ability to harvest rainwater. Even on a balcony, it is possible to do so. Rain barrels come in all different shapes and sizes to fit into every space. It can be as simple as a bucket or tub left outside to fill. It all counts.

To maximize how much you can harvest, you want to be thinking roof, greenhouse, or guttering surface area. The more you can access, the more water you will reap every time it rains. Vessels range from slimline barrels, which can be slipped in discreetly, to heavy-duty multi-chamber containers that can hold 1,200 gallons (4,500 L) or more. Underground containers/cisterns can be used to further maximize home supply if you have the space and money to install them.

Savvy Tip: Don't forget to try to cover your rainwater once it has been collected. Otherwise leaves and twigs can find their way in and that can clog up the taps.

Thrifty Options

Some of the more inexpensive options available for collecting rainwater involve sourcing containers that can be used to house rainwater. You do need to be careful when selecting these vessels. Find out what have been used for previously; the last thing you want is any chemical contamination in your precious water supply.

That said, from repurposed food supply containers to bins to old water tank barrels, try to work with what you can find and make your supply your own, literally.

To Maximize Harvesting

Always cover water barrels to keep twigs and leaves out. I leave one open for the garden birds as they love drinking from it. Just be sure to follow local rules and laws about rain barrel placement and coverings.

Try collecting rainwater from every available roof or surface, including sheds, homes, and greenhouses. On an allotment or in a community garden you can create a freestanding unit with sheet metal on a simple frame to create a shelter that can be used to harvest water into the barrels beneath.

↑ Leaves and debris will collect in an uncovered water barrel, which can cause problems.

KIM'S TIPS

Don't Forget All-Important Gray Water Harvesting

Water from your home has a potential second use in helping to keep your garden quenched during times of heat and water shortage. For example, shower or bath water in particular is a good option. You just need to be mindful about any soap products used because they can be contaminated with non-organic-friendly matter and the reuse is banned in some areas. Cooking water is a safer bet as it has only been used to boil vegetables or grains.

How Much Water Can Be Harvested?

To give you an idea of how much water can be harvesting from rainfall, a regularly used guideline is: 1 inch of rainfall harvested from a 1,000-square-foot (93 sq m) roof yields 600 gallons (2,271 L) of water.

Surprising Water Harvesting Fact

There are states in America where support for rainwater harvesting hasn't been high. For example, it was illegal to harvest rain in California up to about a decade ago when the Rainwater Capture Act was passed.

Container Gardening Watering Tips

Pots, hanging baskets, and planters are more vulnerable to drought because with less growing space and soil, they are prone to drying out quickly in the heat of the day. There are things you can do to help reduce watering requirements and boost resilience in container plantings.

- **Water well and deeply.** Avoid light watering as this will just encourage plants to develop shallow root systems that make plants more vulnerable to the elements.

- **Consider watering from underneath** (bottom watering).

- **Go a bit deeper on the mulching.** Mulches really are one of your biggest allies; they can help keep that precious water in the ground for longer to protect your plants.

- **Spent potting mix** from other planting pots can be used as an impromptu mulch.

- **Move your pots** to an area with partial shade during a heatwave to help them cope. Create a temporary shade screen for too-heavy-to-move-containers. Anything that creates shade is fine. Be creative with what you can find: An old door, other tall plants, or even a bed sheet may work well.

Compost and leaf mold are better for pots and containers, but if you can get your savvy green fingers on any wool, then this is an amazing material to work with. It can be homestead sheep's wool or old woolen clothing—wherever this resource might be available. Wool helps hold moisture in the soil beautifully. One of the main peat-free compost brands in the United Kingdom, Dalefoot, uses wool as a main ingredient in their mixes for good reasons. You can line hanging baskets with it and use it as a mulch over the top. It really helps. I've experimented before with growing a super water-hungry squash in a small hanging basket that was lined with wool. I did not water at all to see how it would fare, and it still managed to produce some fruit.

← Make the best use of container space and help keep moisture in.

5 Save Money While Saving the Planet by Recycling and Repurposing

How to transform waste into wonderous gardening materials.

CLIMATE CHANGE IS OVERWHELMING and immensely anxiety inducing. Knowing that all these changes are coming, and that the powers-that-be don't seem to be doing enough, it can all feel out of control and frankly scary. Yet, we can help make a difference and take positive action one waste material at a time by being part of the solution, instead of part of the problem.

Rather than throwing something away, think: Can this be fixed or put to some other use instead? Nail the raised beds that have come loose back into place. Clean a rusty pair of secateurs with wire wool, then sharpen and oil them. Turn an old plastic bottle into a protective plant cloche by cutting it in half. Take old, out-of-date lettuce seed packets and germinate them for pick-and-come-again leaves. Transform an old kitchen garbage bin into a herbarium.

Recycling and repurposing relies on the process of problem solving. Figuring out how to mend or upcycle a broken item builds confidence, and it feels important and good.

← An old trug has been turned into a windowsill vegetable garden.

My Own Make, Mend, and Do Journey

My experiences of gardening-for-free many years back for *The Guardian* were invaluable, empowering, and incredibly humbling in equal measure. No- or low-cost gardening wasn't a lesser option by any means. As well as saving money, I was helping to save the planet by greatly reducing the amount of stuff I consumed.

I used less plastic and had a lower carbon footprint, yet there was so much more opportunity to take my gardening onto whole new levels of meaningful sustainability. Ethical, organic, and eco purchasing practices are all well and good, but it's still consuming. This was even better than that. This was minimal purchasing. It was turning items that would otherwise be discarded, or even worse sent to landfill, and finding creative ways to put them to good use, enabling them to continue on.

No single-use or disposable items here. This felt (and still feels today) like a massive, important stride forward and a big part of the climate change–savvy gardening solution.

→ **RIGHT, FROM TOP** An old kitchen bin turned into an herbarium

Making your own compost and leaf mold feels incredibly good.

Why Less Is Simply More

We have become far too used to buying in everything we need, with every possible tool and widget available to buy at any time of the day and just an online delivery service away. Gardening has become far too much about expense. About this perception that we need multifarious tools and gadgets in order to garden well, when in reality vegetable gardens can be nurtured with very little cost investment overall.

Vegetable Gardens Can Be Set Up from Scratch with Very Little Cost

So many expensive items in your average garden center are simply surplus, not requirements. From synthetic weed and bug killers to fancy soil improvers to leaf blowers and a number of products we are led to believe are important. In the climate change–savvy

KIM'S TIPS

The Fight Back Against Our Reliance on Material Objects

Real, deep-down resilience cannot be bought. Yes, there are good-quality tools, seeds, and er . . . books to help you on your hardier gardening way. But learning to improvise and not be so reliant on objects is key. It's important for the sake of the planet, and it's important for your confidence and empowerment to make decisions for yourself and not follow gardening "rules" verbatim. Plus, it feels so incredibly good.

This doesn't mean don't buy anything at all if you can afford it. That's not realistic or indeed fun to be scrabbling around trying to salvage or save seeds from everything you grow if you don't have to. However, less "stuff" is often more when it comes to being resilient in the garden. This low-cost approach helps to make gardening much more accessible to all, which is incredibly important for more sustainable cities and food security for the future.

vegetable garden these are all unnecessary, because natural pest control, soil improvers, and materials are king. Biodiversity is also incredibly important and organic, chemical, pesticide- and peat-free local resources rule the day.

REMEMBER, IT HASN'T ALWAYS BEEN THE CONSUMERISM-LADEN WAY

This perception of need (and cost) is a relatively recent addition to the gardening calendar. Folks used to repair, recycle, swap, barter, and make things from scratch not that long ago, before there were so many products and gardening purchasing options at our disposal. Convenience is nice, but it doesn't foster resilience when everything is just a click away.

- Your garden hose gets a leak—click to buy another one.
- The wheelbarrow wheel has fallen off—click replacement.
- The secateurs have got blunt—click and here are some more.
- I've got a few aphids on my tomato plant—click pest control.

The Problem with Plastic

Disposable items are the bane of the responsible gardener, and nothing screams disposable more than the single-use plastic items that garden centers are generally awash with. From one-use labels and poorly produced (flimsy) pots to cheap tools and everything else in between, despite recent awareness of the problems with plastic, this material is still everywhere.

David Attenborough's eleven *Blue Planet* documentaries really brought the issue into the public domain with its focus on the damage this material is having in the world's oceans and for the many creatures living within. The questions around how much recycling actually ends up being turned into something useful versus how much of it is shipped abroad and ends up in the sea is disturbing. The concerns around how long these materials take to break down and how micro plastics have found their way into so much of the ocean food chain and to the farthest reaches of our planet are very real.

There have been improvements, thankfully, although it's important to be mindful of how planet-friendly some of the plastic-free alternatives actually are. For example, I'm aware of plastic-free pots that contain peat or formaldehyde, which in my mind is hardly an improvement, so it's important to check the provenance of what you are purchasing when something is labeled as a plastic alternative.

. . . and on it goes. A quick-fix solution in the short term—however fair trade or organic it may be—can still be part of the problem by creating more waste items that will be sent to landfill. Yet with just a quick look on Google you'll find that there are many simple repair options for gardening items like this, from glues, repair tape, and new parts that can keep items in use for longer. Keeping these items "alive" produces an incredible feel-good factor to the fixer, builds confidence, and creates a lovely sense of meaningful achievement.

SAVVY INSPIRATION—MAKE YOUR OWN COMPOST

This is one of the easiest and surefire best ways to tap into your inner resilient gardener. The pleasure of making compost for yourself out of waste materials from the garden, kitchen, and elsewhere is down-to-earth perfection. It is easy to do in basically any garden space with lots of different compost bin options, shapes, and sizes. It is a total resilient gardener must.

When I run courses on climate change–savvy gardening, I could talk about compost for hours as there is so much to say about the benefits of making at least some of your own

↓ **BELOW, FROM LEFT**
Turn leftovers into gardeners' gold.

Make your own compost bin.

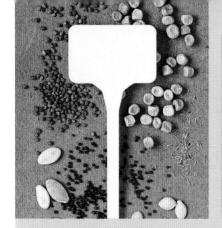

Let's Start with Ditching the Disposable Plastic

Rather than not using plastic materials at all, I work with recycled plastic and help ensure materials that have been produced are kept in active, viable use. The ways I do this include:

- **Polytunnel skins and other essentials:** I look after mine and currently have one that is fourteen-plus years old. They are supposed to only last four to five years before being replaced. Materials such as micro mesh can be used for many years, just by looking after them.

- **Pots:** I reuse plastic pots for many years and salvage old pots to keep them in use. When they are cracked, I repair them with duct tape, basic but effective to keep them out of the landfill.

- **Plastic bottles:** I salvage these and cut them up to make protective cloches for plants. Just store them away for use early and late in the season.

- **Plastic labels:** Just clean them off with vinegar and reuse them for many seasons.

- **DIY compost and soil amendments:** Eliminate the plastic bags from purchased potting soils and composts by making your own soil improvers and buying in bulk.

- **Make your own plants:** Rather than buying plants, I sow from seed and take cuttings when possible. Start small at first and build your confidence over time.

- **Use old toilet roll middles to sow seeds:** Make your own tiny pots for seed starting. The seedling and biodegradable pot can then be planted out whole.

There are so many ways to transform other waste plastic materials into longer-term, useful service. Make a wildlife pond out of a plastic sink basin, or try turning spent garden boots (Wellies) into attractive and novel planters.

↑ **ABOVE, FROM LEFT** Clean and reuse plastic plant labels.

The plastic skin on this polytunnel is fourteen-plus years old and still going strong.

homemade "gardener's gold." In an organic gardening system, healthy soil is king, queen, and everything in between. Get this right and it will boost the health and vitality of all of your plants. Compost is the best soil improver going. It feeds plants and encourages micro-organisms in the soil. It helps the ground hold onto and absorb more water and it improves its structure. No matter your soil type—compost is generally the best cure-all.

This amazing material is incredibly easy to make even in the smallest of outside spaces because there are many different shaped and sized compost bins on the market, so there's bound to be something that works for you.

The confidence building and satisfaction that comes with the creation of this prized material is also worth its weight in gold. When it comes to building resilience in the garden (and the gardener), it's simply one of the best things you can do. As well as saving money through the creation of your own supply of soil improver, in the process you will be complicit in the magical journey of waste slowly but surely being turned into something useful and indeed, incredibly special.

↓ **BELOW, FROM LEFT**
Make your own leaf mold with this fabulous free material, and add it as an ingredient to the compost pile.

Add comfrey to supercharge your compost pile.

SAVE MONEY WHILE SAVING THE PLANET BY RECYCLING AND REPURPOSING

Reasons to Make Compost

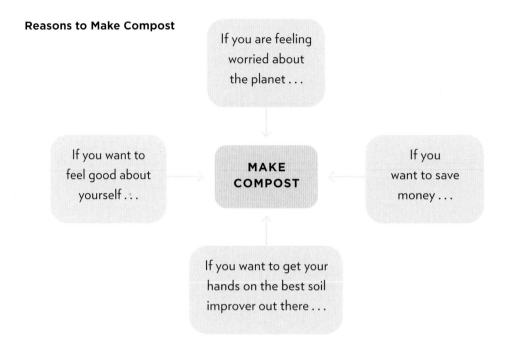

The Basic Ingredients for a Cold Composting System

- A roughly equal mix of brown and green materials
- Vegetable or fruit peelings from the kitchen
- Cereal or tea packets, or cardboard: Just remove any staples or tape. Most inks used today are vegetable-based, so no need to keep printed items out of the compost bin.
- Egg shells: You can bake them on a low heat in the oven to dry them first, but it's not essential.
- Coffee or tea leaves
- Leaves from the trees
- Wood chips
- Spent chicken house bedding: This is a great compost accelerator!
- Ash from a wood fire
- Clippings from the garden: It's best to cut it up a bit first if branches are thick.
- Old plants: It is fine if they are diseased or insect nibbled.
- Seaweed if there is a beach near to you
- Farmyard animal manure: Just mix it in to supercharge your pile.

- Comfrey: You can add a few harvests from just one plant each year—it's amazing stuff.
- Borage, stinging nettles, and other "green" plant materials: Just try to avoid any seeds, though.
- Grass clippings: Add only a thin layer. It you add too much, the compost can become anaerobic (i.e., go bad).
- Natural clothing materials, including wool or cotton: Cut it up and add it in.

COLD COMPOSTING OPTIONS

Plastic Bins

Stalwart plastic bins can be easily squeezed into a corner somewhere and will dutifully break down your scraps and produce a decent quantity of compost. Standard bins are larger and generally cheaper to buy, but there also are many different space-saving options available nowadays that are suitable for patio or balcony gardens.

Hot Bins

These more elaborate, sometimes rotating, composting systems raise the temperature of the contents to a sufficient level so that even meat and cooked ingredients can be added and reliably broken down. They also tend to work more quickly than your standard cold composting system. They do cost more to buy however, so if they are out of your budget, you can opt to make a hot compost heap instead of containing it in a bin if you have the space. Ideally a hot compost heap should be at least 4 feet square (1.2 m²) in size. The pile will also need to be turned regularly to help fire-up the microbial activity inside the pile and speed up decomposition.

Homemade Bins

Ultimately, open-chamber bins, which can be made from salvaged materials such as old pallets or wire fencing, work incredibly well. Pallets can be sourced for free from builders' yards and shaped to fit the space you have in mind. They are also rather lovely to work with. I have a four-chamber, pallet-based compost bin and can more easily turn the contents of

What Can't You Add In?

Anything cooked should not be added to a cold composting system—oils contained in it will not break down. Also, it will most likely attract rodents.

Whole weeds with roots or seed heads should not be added. You can soak them in a bucket of water for a couple of months to kill them and then add in if you'd like.

Anything plastic or materials that will not biodegrade should not go in your compost system. Be careful to remove anything unsuitable as you pile on your ingredients.

one bin into another to speed up the decomposition process. It also enables me to maximize the amount of compost I can reliably make with more chambers in which to work.

You can make bins out of salvaged sheet metal or whatever wood you can get your hands on. I've even seen fantastic bays made from part of an old bed frame.

Wormeries

This can be nice project for a school or home educational project for children as these systems are designed to house, feed, and farm a whole host of worms. You add layered ingredients as you would do in a standard compost bin, but you have to be extra robust with the mixture to create the best, more balanced environment possibly for your resident worms. For example, you have to be careful with citrus—you can add a bit but not too much.

Commercially made vermicomposting systems come with a tap at the bottom that collects and delivers the liquid produced from your system and that many package up as "worm tea"—a most effective fertilizer to be added to your vegetable patch to boost homegrown results.

Of course, worms will be active and present in most ground-touching compost systems anyway, so personally I prefer to work with worms in this way instead. It also highlights the benefits of heathy soil in your garden overall; it should be alive with worms that will be "making tea" and aerating the soil on your behalf in a free-range, low-maintenance way.

Tips for Success

- **If you can situate your compost bin** so it is touching the soil, the earthworms and the many creatures involved in the process of compost making can find their way in to lend a helping hand.

- **Turning the pile is helpful** and will help warm it up to speed decomposition along nicely. Alternatively, you can add alternate layers of finished compost within the other layers to boost results and encourage the microorganisms to better work their way through.

- **Use compost accelerator materials** such as comfrey, nettles, and chicken manure and bedding if you can access a supply.

- **Make your compost pile supercharged** by adding a diversity of ingredients to the mix. I do this rather than making or using any separate fertilizer.

HOW TO MAKE LEAF MOLD

You can use a dedicated container to make leaf mold, but I would recommend that it be open to the elements as this helps with the process of decomposition. I use one of the chambers of my compost bin, and also leave layers of leaves to rot down under the shelter of trees scattered around my gardens. Once the leaves are collected together, just let nature work its magic until spring when you can remove the top layer of undecomposed leaves (ideally with your hands) to get to the lovely crumbly fully decomposed material underneath, which of course, is called leaf mold.

It really is that simple.

← A pile of leaf litter naturally breaks down into leaf mold under the shelter of a small tree.

Using Leaf Mold As a Seed-Starting Medium for Free

Although some people know that leaf mold makes a fab seed-starting medium, convoluted recipes are, again, the order of the day, with "20 percent of this mixed with blah, blah 10 percent of that," then finally add the leaf mold. But the truth of the matter is much simpler and a perfect testimony to the fact that nature knows best and doesn't bother with such exacting nonsense.

What happens in the woods? Leaves fall from the trees to the ground and decompose in thin layers, which means decomposition tends to be quicker and more robust. Scratch beneath the surface in spring and you find leaf mold from the previous season.

This is why on my journey of gardening-for-free for *The Guardian* I was able to produce my own supply of seed-starting medium by rooting around under trees in the spring (once the insects had finished overwintering) and foraging for this luscious material. After tentatively experimenting with different mixes, I found that just leaf mold alone makes a brilliant seed-starting medium, and no other ingredients are required. Yes, you might get the odd weed seed germinating in your trays, and do watch out for slug eggs, but otherwise the results were on par with a good-quality bagged seed-starting product.

Savvy Tip: If you have any mole hills in your homestead or garden, then this is one ingredient I would recommend be mixed into your lovely crumbly leaf mold. It's free. It's fantastic. And it's a local resource that can be put to good use.

↑ Use leaf mold as a seed-starting medium.

Also leaving ramshackle piles of leaves around your garden or allotment edges has a massive benefit for wildlife over winter. Predators such as ground beetles, amphibians, and many others will be able to seek shelter, while birds love to rummage through piles in search of juicy insects.

Other Uses for Leaf Mold

This material that falls freely from nearby trees in autumn can be put to a number of great uses. It is a fantastic soil improver that can be added to beds alongside compost in the spring. It seems to really encourage earthworm activity.

Your stock of leaf mold also comes to the rescue in the summer months when it can be used as a mulch around water-hungry plants to help keep the water in the ground and reduce the amount of to-and-fro watering required by you. This works well in both open beds and for potted plants alike.

Perhaps most excitingly, leaf mold can be used as a seed-starting mix. See the sidebar on page 92 for more on that.

WONDERFUL WOOD CHIPS

This is another fantastic material that can be sourced for free if you have the space to house a pile or two. Tree surgeons or local electricity companies doing work in your area are the best bet for supply as they are often keen to find somewhere to offload the leftovers of their work.

This natural material has many uses, including as a thin mulch around plants to help keep moisture in. There is more on how to do this on page 73. Wood chips also are a useful addition to the compost heap, as a covering for pathways, and if it's left to rot down for three to four years, it also transforms into a superb no-cost seed-starting medium to boot. Plus, as if that wasn't enough, it also can be used for growing mushrooms.

KEEP TOOLS IN USE FOR LONGER

If good-quality tools can be repaired and given some yearly love, they can become the only tools you need, year in, year out. Secateurs will go rusty at the end of the growing season if left alone because any plant residue left on it can gum it up. A spade's edge or

---

GARDEN PROJECT

Furniture Fantastic

Old chests, drawers, chairs, or even sideboards that are destined for the dump can be repurposed to make attractive planters for your home or garden. Old ceramic sinks, toilet bowls, too. With the addition of some compost and plants, they can make a meaningful feature in your growing space.

lawn mower blades can become blunt and not work as effectively. Rather than replacing items like these, here's how to look after your tools so they save you money and look after your climate change–resilient vegetable garden in exchange.

A spray with WD-40, a rub with sandpaper, and a few minutes with a sharpening stone followed by an oiling will bring most pairs of secateurs back into full service. Spades can equally be sharpened with a stone for maximum effectiveness. Store tools somewhere dry and out of the rain to minimize rusting.

GARDEN PROJECT

Make Your Own Cold Frame

Old windows and shower doors are normally sent straight to the landfill no questions asked—yet they make fantastic lids for a homemade cold frame. You can get your resilient gardener paws on these fantastic free materials by looking for building renovation projects in your area or by speaking to remodeling companies or asking at your local community refuse site.

Don't be shy. If you don't ask, you don't get. And people will likely be intrigued and impressed with your rescuing of these otherwise disposable items.

You can then make (and use) your cold frame in a number of different ways. If you have existing raised beds, it's possible your lids could be used on top to provide protection for plants early and late in the season, creating a mini greenhouse.

A standalone cold frame can be made out of materials you might have on hand. If you have an old box or chest, the lid can be removed and replaced with your upcycled window or shower door. Likewise, repurposed bricks or wood can be used to make a frame for your lid. If the window or shower door can be attached by a latch, that's great, if not, don't worry; it can simply be secured in place with a brick or two on top. It all works just the same.

↑ I'm turning an old window into an impromptu cold frame to protect plants over winter.

GARDEN PROJECT

DIY Propagators

To give your seedlings a helping hand, a propagator is an incredibly useful tool. It helps raise the temperature to encourage seeds to germinate in the first place, and it can provide valuable all-weather protection to seedlings early and late in the year.

Here are some ideas to make your own. I'm sure there are plenty more materials that could be repurposed in this way, so get creative with whatever you can find. It's fun, it's free, and it's incredibly future thinking.

- Large water bottles can be cut in two around the middle to create a lift-up propagator for plants.

- Old, clear plastic, supermarket produce trays can be doubled up (one on top of the other) to create mini under-cover homes for seedlings.

- Clear plastic storage boxes can work well. Just place some boxes (or bricks) inside to raise your seed trays up higher, then cover the box with a translucent lid to allow light in. Clear plastic food wrap would work well as a cover and a lot of shop or online-purchased items come covered in the stuff, so using it in this meaningful way prevents it from being single use.

- Plastic bottles can be cut in two and turned into two mini cloches to protect small plants.

↑ Plastic bottle cloche

KIM'S TIP

Tips for Success and Safety

It's best to make a few drainage holes in your planters at the bottom.

When choosing subjects for planters, it's important to work with materials that don't contain any nasty chemicals, so wood, stone, ceramic, and basic plastic are safe. Do be careful with peeling paint on wood, or anything with lead or unknown materials. If you salvage any containers from agricultural settings, check that they haven't been used to house nasty chemicals first. Other than that, it's mainly down to common sense.

GARDEN PROJECT

Makeshift Planter Ideas

Here's where you can really get creative because there are so many salvageable items that can be turned into beautiful, no-cost planters for your resilient vegetable garden. Start by having a look around your home for inspiration, and as you build confidence you can spread your repurposing wings further afield. You'll be amazed by what people throw out. One person's waste is another's wondrous windowsill garden.

→ **RIGHT, FROM TOP** Plastic pots make good windowsill planters.
Get creative with planters. It feels good to repurpose.

GARDEN PROJECT

Hanging Baskets

That old colander you picked up in a charity shop but haven't used yet would make a great hanging basket after lining it first so the soil doesn't leach away. Old plastic sheeting with a few drainage holes makes a good liner. To help with water retention, any natural wool items can work wonders as well. If you can get your hands on any sheep wool from homesteaders, a thin layer inside will make all the difference. That moth-damaged sweater you have at the back of the cupboard—also perfect.

To hang your basket, even simple string or ribbon can work well, or you can reuse chain from an old hanging basket, or use whatever you can get your hands on.

← **FROM LEFT** This cold frame for seedlings is made out of an old window.

Get creative with your growing spaces.

SAVVY PROJECT IDEAS TO PROVIDE PROTECTION, NO MATTER THE WEATHER

With our changing climate and erratic seasons, one of the biggest risks early in the year is a temperature plummet after we've all got started sowing seeds, thinking spring was well and truly underway. So having protection on hand to mitigate any sudden temperature drop is incredibly important. The good news is you can do so for free.

Get Inspired

Once you start along this path, the ideas will flow and you'll no longer look at so-called rubbish in the same way. Those boots that have a hole in the bottom—why not transform them into an herb garden for your back door? That handbag that has a broken zipper— what a great hanging basket to hang on the apple tree in your yard. Those plastic bottles you found dumped down your street—why not cut them in half and add them to your pile of pots?

GROWING ON FROM SUPERMARKET LEFTOVERS

As well as composting much of your kitchen and home leftovers, there are many potential house and garden plants that can be regrown from scraps. There are more growing recommendations on page 99, but here are a few ideas to get excited about.

Supermarket Herb Pots

Anyone who has bought these plastic encased herbs from a grocery store will know that soon after purchase they invariably die, promoting the purchase of another to take their place. These are a perfect example of the quick-fix culture of gardening that encourages time, effort, and money in the pursuit of edibles, when in fact these battery herb pots (as I call them) can be saved and planted out and on for multiple harvesting opportunities ahead.

Why not rescue one of these plants next time you see one in a store? Simply remove the herb plant (thyme, chives, basil, parsley, and cilantro/coriander) from its pot and look at what lies underneath. You're most likely to find a heavily compacted root ball with many seedlings packed into a small space and very little growing medium remaining. That explains why they die so readily and quickly when brought home.

Saving these plants and turning them into viable crops is therefore an incredibly positive action to take. As well as bagging yourself multiple plants in the process, you also are taking a stand against this unsustainable cycle of consumption.

Take your battery herb pot out of its container. Carefully feeling your way around the roots, divide it onto five or more plants. Plant each one into a separate pot with room to grow. The plant may be slightly stressed at first, but cutting it back will help conserve its strength, enabling it to grow into its new home, free from its previously confined quarters.

Lemongrass

This aromatic plant is a vital ingredient in Thai cooking, and packets of stems are commonly found in many supermarkets. They are rather expensive to buy but actually fairly easy to grow for yourself. Take some of the shop-bought stems before they go to waste and place them in a glass of water on a warm, sunny-as-you-can windowsill. Change the water every few days. Over time (quicker in spring and summer) they will slowly but surely attempt to grow up and out the top of the stem, as thin roots begin to emerge from the base of the stem. Once they've sprouted new growth, it's time to plant them onto a pot of their own in good-quality, peat-free multipurpose growing medium. Keep the pots inside until they become further established.

These plants can be kept outside during the later spring and summer, then brought back inside over winter as they are frost sensitive. That said, when I was living in Brighton I had a lemongrass plant outside in an herb rockery that happily stood firm over winter for a number of years.

Ginger and Turmeric

So incredibly good for you and perfectly feasible to grow for yourself, these flavorsome and anti-inflammatory stems are an easy must. Choose a piece of ginger or turmeric (roughly a couple of inches in size) with a visible eye (the protruding, knobby piece) and place it in a reusable plastic sandwich bag on a kitchen window. The added heat and moisture encourage sprouting and watch as a green shoot starts to emerge from the eye. This indicates it's ready to plant out in your pot of choice.

Again, keep turmeric or ginger plants inside and grow them as an edible houseplant in spring. Move them outdoors for the summer before harvesting later in the season.

ADVENTURES WITH SUPERMARKET LEFTOVERS

You'll be surprised how much opportunity there is for plant creation from the average supermarket basket and there is resilience to be found therein. Of course, not all produce can be transformed into viable, edible plants. You aren't going to grow pineapples or avocados in your back garden in most parts of the world, but they do make very attractive and rewarding houseplants. If you're lucky enough to live in a warm climate with no

GARDEN PROJECT

Recycled Raised Beds

My raised beds are made out of wood leftover from building projects such as timber joists. Viable beds can be made out anything from stone, brick, or galvanized metal, as well as reclaimed wood. Just try to avoid any wood that has paint or is showing signs of decay.

SAVE MONEY WHILE SAVING THE PLANET BY RECYCLING AND REPURPOSING

GARDEN PROJECT

Growing an Indoor Mushroom Kit

There are lots of ready-to-grow kits on the market that provide a few flushes of delicious mushrooms and then that's it. You might be surprised to learn that you can keep them alive to carry on producing, especially in the case of oyster mushroom. They are very easy to work with because they simply love growing on so many different materials.

After your kit stops producing, remove the white spongy material from inside (that's your mycelium), which is the living fungi that produces the fruiting bodies (which are your delicious mushrooms). It's not dead when it's finished fruiting mushrooms; it just needs more food to have the energy to spread and grow on. It is much like a seedling that has outgrown its pot and become root bound; your mycelium needs a bigger space and more food.

The good news with oyster mushrooms is that they aren't that fussy. From coffee grounds and straw to wood chips, compost, leaf mold, wool, cardboard, old books, or even natural fibers such as denim—they are really unfussy eaters.

To continue growing oyster mushrooms, simply break up your lump of mycelium into two or four pieces and place the broken-up chunks in your new growing medium. Wood chips and coffee grounds are two of the easiest to work with. In the case of wood chips, it's a good idea to sterilize them first by heating on low in a pot to help kill any other fungi spores

that might be otherwise present. Coffee grounds can be used as is. You might find it hard to keep up supply from your coffee drinking alone, however. Unless you like the idea of having an excuse to drink more coffee "because the fungi need it," your local coffee shop can provide a good additional source if you ask them for leftovers.

Beyond the growing medium, you'll need a container. Grow your oyster mushrooms in anything from old bread bins and plastic containers to pots. Some form of clear lid is advisable to keep out flies. You also can sometimes see mycelium on the stalks of supermarket-bought mushrooms. You can plant that as well. Magic.

↑ Grow your own fantastic fungi—oyster mushrooms.

frost, you can grow these plants in your back garden. Here are some other ways to reap edible rewards from what would otherwise be discarded.

Plums and Apricots

Many fruits (such as apples and pears) are unreliable to grow from the seeds inside of store-bought fruit because you don't know quite what you will end up with. If you have lots of space, give it a whirl, but a more reliable exercise is the growing of plum and apricot stones.

Save your stones over winter and plant them in a pot outside so they can experience the cold of winter before hopefully springing into life in spring. This is the lowest maintenance option.

I prefer to replicate what would happen naturally—fruit falls from the trees at the end of the season and saplings emerge from the ground nearby as a result.

Tomatoes, Peppers, and Chilies

You can save seeds from these plants, dry them, and attempt to grow them the following spring. It is best, though, to grow from organic, non-F1 varieties to be sure of what you are growing, so opt for heritage varieties. I have included more examples in the chapter on growing under cover for indoor edibles overwintering ideas and inspiration on page 184.

GET CONNECTED

To fully maximize your opportunities for no-cost and less-waste planet-friendly gardening, it's important to reach out within your local community. Doing so opens up opportunities for good old-fashioned and fun swaps, bartering, and exchanges. Whether it is seed-swapping events, the borrowing and sharing of tools, or finding out about freecycle items available in your neighborhood, there is power in people. The more we can work together, the more opportunities there will be to support and share with each other.

I know I keep saying it, but we really are all in this together.

6 Breed and Propagate Locally Resilient Plants

How to select the best, most resilient plant traits for your specific climate.

← Letting plants go to seed provides me with lots of seedlings for free for myself and people in my courses, and to give away to friends and family.

ONE OF THE BEST, MOST ENRICHING, resilient activities you can undertake for the future is the home- and community-saving and sharing of seed. One silver lining of all we have been through these past few years is that more gardeners across the world have discovered the benefits of allowing plants to grow on for seed saving. Whether the reason is for money saving, for food security, for biodiversity boosting, or for love, seed saving has so many benefits.

The real question is why wouldn't you want to tap into some of these home-saved capsules of hope for the future? Home seed saving produces seed that is increasingly more adapted to your own area's growing conditions, therefore boosting resilience. In addition to this, you can further hone the best plant traits by saving seed from produce that has shown the best performance in extreme weather conditions (e.g., drought or heat). This, in turn, enables you to help create super-resilient seed that is tailor-made for your plot and likely will be better able to stand firm against the many extremes outlined in the pages of this book.

It's a climate change–savvy gardener must.

Seed Security Concerns

During the beginning of the COVID-19 pandemic, there was such a surge in sales of fruit and vegetable seed that online retailers struggled. Websites crashed with the sheer volume of traffic and supplies dwindled. What this tsunami of interest in home vegetable gardening during the first lockdown did was shine a spotlight on the potential for home seed saving as a positive action for climate change. No matter what is happening in the world and where seed supplies happen to be, you will have some of your own stock of next years' produce-to-be safely in hand.

Know also that because the genetic diversity of seed has dwindled significantly over the years with mostly commercially available varieties as our main go-to options, this causes massive vulnerability for the future. It means that we are reliant on this small number of crops and many of them will struggle as the weather extremes really start to kick in, which, in many parts of the world, is already happening. Yet there is opportunity and hope in older, more locally adapted varieties that we can make available within our communities at large. Seed saving matters tremendously on both a local and global scale.

↑ I participate in many seed-saving activities.

Let's Get Seedy

Even saving seed from a couple of types of produce each year is enormously beneficial. You wouldn't want to save seed from everything you grow, as doing so would be time intensive and indeed not much fun. This is where local seed-swap events and community engagement come into their own. Join a local gardening group or an organic farming or permaculture club and share the seed-saving love with others. Some good old-fashioned exchange and barter goes a long way. It's fun, and it's rewarding. And remember that the

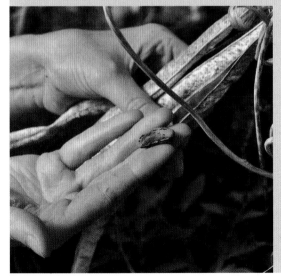

A Rich History of Seed Sovereignty

Of course there's nothing new about any of this. Yet again it's old knowledge that needs to come back full circle. There is a rich heritage and connection that comes with home-saving seed. It used to be a firm part of the yearly gardening calendar before we all got so used to buying everything in. Many families have saved seed through generations (Aunty Nora's Broad Beans . . .), and there is a history and connection with communities and the past and present that is rich and important.

In many countries and cultures, the saving of seed from the annual crops is seen as scared. Seed is life. For food, for future generations . . . and the practices are intermingled in community practices and ancient and spiritual wisdom. Wherever we live, we are all custodians of our land and potential guardians of seed and its security and sacred sovereignty.

← **LEFT, FROM TOP** I allow Welsh poppies to self-seed with gusto for biodiversity and just because.

People used to save seed as part of the gardening calendar.

↑ Seed matters. There's abundant seed from a lettuce plant if you let it go to flower.

more you can connect and collaborate, the more resilient you will be, and the better you will feel all around, guaranteed.

THE EASIEST PLANTS FROM WHICH TO SAVE SEED

Peas

These little beauties are among the best for beginners as they are incredibly straightforward to work with. Just allow a few pods to fatten on the plant. Then, either leave them on the plant until they start to go slightly yellow or pick them when the pods are plump and green, before removing the seeds and placing them somewhere to fully dry. A warm spot indoors, such as a windowsill, is perfect. Once dry, the pea seeds can be stored away. More on how to do that in a bit.

Lettuce

You don't tend to get that much seed in packets of salad greens nowadays, certainly not when you like to grow a lot of these luscious leaves for pick-and-come-again opportunities, as I do. Saving your own lettuce seeds affords you with a diverse and plentiful supply. Just allow a few plants to mature and flower, which happens when they grow tall and burst into flower (bolting). This looks different for each variety of lettuce and do make sure you don't save seed from plants that shoot up and flower almost immediately, as this indicates a bolting tendency, which is something you don't want to encourage in future generations.

Lettuce is easy when it comes to saving seeds. The only challenge is in a wet summer when the seed heads might rot on the plants if there is a lot of rain. Pot-grown plants can be brought inside for seed saving instead in this instance or remove seed heads as early as you can to allow them to dry inside before they can rot. The blooms also make attractive cut flowers or edible decorations for food.

Rocket/Arugula

This plucky, peppery plant will spread with abandon when given the chance, and the flowers are also edible and attractive to boot. They are great for attracting pollinators on your plot, so do allow some to flower even if you don't plan to save seed from them. Once the seed has set, you can either remove it and allow it to dry indoors before storing away, or sprinkle some seeds on the ground outside so that it self-sows and spreads au naturel. I use rocket as ground cover around other plants in the veggie plot. Again, try to avoid saving from a plant that has gone to seed quickly.

Radish

A zesty taste of summer and a super fine fast grower, these roots are an invaluable veg patch must. They are easy to save seed from, just by allowing a few plants to mature and flower. The long seedpods can be easily dried and saved.

↓ **BELOW, FROM TOP**
A lettuce plant as it flowers before turning to seed

Radish produces the most gorgeous flowers that also are edible.

BREED AND PROPAGATE LOCALLY RESILIENT PLANTS

↑ **ABOVE, FROM TOP**
Tomatoes are easy to save seed from, especially the low-fuss way.

Self-seeded parsley in gravel

Tomatoes

If you have a greenhouse or polytunnel, you will undoubtedly have experienced some self-seeding tomatoes from the previous year's windfall. It used to be an old market gardener's trick to just bury a few tomatoes in the ground so the seeds could germinate and spring into life the following year, producing lots of seedlings to be removed and planted out elsewhere.

To save your tomato seeds in a more deliberate fashion, just remove (or eat!) the luscious flesh and remove the seed and its jellylike surround. Common advice dictates that you need to add your seed to a jar of water to allow the surrounding material to ferment and break away from the seed, which can then be removed and dried. Personally, I find that unnecessary. Instead, I either leave the seed on a windowsill to dry or spread it out on a bit of cardboard to dry before cutting the cardboard up and storing it away with the seed attached to it. The cardboard is biodegradable anyway and it all breaks down after planting, so either option works perfectly well.

Parsley

Parsley is one of my favorite herbs to grow, thanks to so many delicious uses in the kitchen, but it can be a bit tricky to germinate from packet seed. If, however, you let your plant grow on into its second year, as a biennial, it will attempt to flower and set seed. In doing so, you will bag yourself lots of luscious plants for free. You can either collect the seeds or allow them to drop onto the surrounding soil where they will germinate at the appropriate time. This ample seedling supply can be dug up and transplanted around your garden or passed on to others.

Chilies/Peppers

Although these plants can potentially cross-pollinate with other varieties that are growing nearby (meaning that if you are growing two different varieties of peppers and you save seeds, you might end up with a mix of traits from both), you will still end up with something worth growing. In the case of chilies, they tend to just get hotter in terms of flavor, so if you like hot chilies, then you will probably like this. You also can come up with a fun name for your supercharged new variety of plant and keep saving from it again if you like it for years to come.

Beans

Beans can be saved easily like peas, just leave some pods on the plants to mature and fatten before removing them when they're yellow. Fully dry the seeds before storing them away.

Cilantro (Coriander)

This lovely zesty herb is great to home-save from, just be careful to pick only the plants that haven't gone quickly to seed. Certainly in the summer months, cilantro/coriander will bolt with abandon, so saving seed is easier earlier or later in the year. Said seeds will then germinate with abandon. Cilantro/coriander can be grown reliably over winter on a windowsill or under cover, so I'd recommend using some of your home-saved supply the same year. Nothing brightens up a bleak winter's evening than an herb-packed meal to impress.

↑ Cilantro/coriander as it goes to seed

KIM'S TIP

A Word on F1

When it comes to saving seed, one important exception is any variety labeled F1. The main reason for this is that the F1 indicates that the plant is a hybrid that has been bred by combining the genetics of two or more different varieties of that plant. This, in turn, means that you don't know what you will end up with if you try to save seed from those hybrid plants. They are not reliable or true-to-type at all, so it is best avoided. Unless you like unpredictable surprises that might not taste or produce very well.

PLANT BREEDING FOR THE BEST RESILIENT TRAITS

Breeding your own varieties is super exciting as it enables you to save seed from the plants that have displayed the best genetic traits you want to encourage. The more you save seed, the more you can hone these traits of choice over the years, and the better, more adapted to your own individual plot the seed will become. This means you are effectively breeding a new generation of super seed that is designed to perform better and more reliably all around, no matter the whatever-the-weather future ahead.

Select from plants that have performed best in terms of productivity, or for size, flavor, and all-around awesomeness. You also can select produce that has fared best against extremes of weather in your area. Whether it's prolonged periods of drought, especially wet weather, or unexpected cold, strong winds, or flooding, some varieties will simply perform better than others. Save from those that show resilience.

As you learned in the previous chapters, how you garden is key. Soil health is everything, and it's also worth noting that not all plants from a batch of seed will perform the same. Home in on those that fared better: Maybe it was plants that were able to stand firm against pest or disease. Or maybe some didn't bolt as quickly as others. These are all positive, resilient traits you want to select for.

→ Fennel seed heads also make lovely cut flowers.

How to Boost the Performance of the Seed You Save at Home

First, be sure your seeds are ready. Wait until the seed has fully ripened on the plant. This means the seed has grown as big as it can grow. In the case of fruits, ensure they have gone overripe. In the case of pods, they should grow fat and start to dry.

When selecting candidates for seed saving, remember:

- Don't save seed from FI plants.
- Choose parent plants that display the best examples of the produce you want to reproduce (e.g., the best looking and tasting peas).
- Avoid weaker-looking or poorly performing plants.
- Make sure seed is fully dry before storing it away.
- Ensure seed is properly stored away without any insects.
- Store seed away from heat in a dry location. Paper envelopes or repurposed old seed packets are best.

↑ Choose the best examples of plant and resilient traits because these are the traits you want to carry on.

For the purpose of genetic diversity, this works best when you act collaboratively with others in your local community, swapping and sharing your produce seed over the years.

MORE ADVANCED SEED SAVING

There are many great books on the subject of home plant breeding and seed saving, if you want to dive in and experiment. Until then, here are more of the best vegetable seeds to save at home, though these varieties are a little more challenging than the last batch and require some particular considerations.

Carrots

Carrots are much easier than you might be led to believe. To save seed from carrots, just follow a few simple rules. You will need at least twenty good-quality roots. Remember choose the best examples of the variety you wish to save. You need so many plants to ensure good genetic diversity in the resulting seed.

↓ **BELOW, FROM LEFT**
Carrot flower heads are also amazing for enhancing insect biodiversity.

Seed saving results in capsules of hope for the future.

Remove the roots in autumn and store them in a box of earth or sand in a cool, dark room that does not freeze. In early spring, remove the roots and plant them out deeply in a bed of your choice. Leave about 1 foot (30 cm) between each root and plant them in a block as they need to be close together to aid in pollination.

Watch that they don't cross with another carrot variety (including wild types—more on those in a bit), which as outbreeders, they would otherwise do. This is pretty straightforward as it happens, because it's unlikely that anyone else will be saving their carrot seed so immediately close by your garden—unless they are reading this book of course!

As biennials, your carrot roots will only attempt to flower and set seed in their second year. Watch out for wild carrots that might be growing nearby and will readily cross-pollinate with your cultivated carrots. Known as Queen Ann's Lace, it has the same feathery fonds as cultivated carrots and grows on wasteland or in fields—although there is research being conducted on the potential resilience of wild and cultivated carrot mixes, so maybe that isn't such a bad thing after all! See page 115 for further information.

As an added plus, carrot flowers are absolutely stunning. They are hugely ornamental, and the resulting seed will be produced in abundance. Be prepared to store it away for many years to come, and you will still have plenty to give away to others for swaps.

Kale and Beets

Of the brassica family, I would say these two are easiest from which to save seed. You can keep harvesting the lovely kale leaves in autumn and straight through winter to spring before they attempt to flower and set seed.

If you live in a reasonably mild climate (or are growing under cover), beets can be left in the ground before allowing them to grow on and set seed in the following spring. Otherwise, beet roots can also be stored like carrots as described above and then planted out again in early spring to mature. Allow about 1 foot (30 cm) between beets ideally and roughly 2 feet (61 cm) between kale plants.

You will need about twenty or more plants.

Both of these are outbreeders again, so this means that they will readily cross with any other member of the brassica family that happens to be flowering at the same time. That might not be a bad thing, as you may create something tasty as a result, but equally, you might not. Keep the seed true-to-type by avoiding crossing to be safe.

Kale and beets will flower and set seed in their second year, and the resulting flowers, which occur in spring, are also great for attracting pollinators to your plot early in the

Jimmy's Chilies

The more you experiment with seed saving, the more your confidence will build and the more exciting opportunities there will be. Swapping seed with others is really fun and provides a connection and a history with your plants and produce, one that store-bought plants or seeds simply cannot match. Right now, one of my favorite varieties of chilies to grow is called Jimmy's Chilies, simply because they came from a colleague of my partner, who, yes, you guessed it, is named Jimmy. They are highly productive bush chili plants that seem to keep growing no matter what you throw at them. Great for containers, they can be brought inside and overwintered. They are the chili that keeps on giving and I have no idea which variety they came from originally, nor does it matter.

→ Super-Resilient Bush Chili—Jimmy's Chilies

season. It's mainly purple sprouting broccoli and broccoli you need to watch out for, but also any mizuna or mibuna that might happen to be left in the ground over winter. Just ensure they flower at separate times and your offspring seed will come true.

Again, be prepared to reap a bountiful reward from your efforts. I still have 'Red Russian' kale germinating in my vegetable beds as a result of seed I saved more than ten years ago. I had so much that I ended up cold composting some, and it popped up as free seedlings in my plot for many years after.

Runner Beans and Broad Beans
These vegetable patch delicacies will cross with other bean varieties growing nearby, so one option, if you want to grow a few varieties, is to stagger your planting to ensure that flowering occurs at different times. They are otherwise very easy seed to save seed from.

BOOSTING BIODIVERSITY

Enabling plants to grow, flower, and set seed is fantastic for natural biodiversity in your outside space. It creates food for pollinators and a range of beneficial creatures, and is an important ally in natural pest control efforts.

→ Mixed plants, such as lettuce, rocket/arugula, fennel, and radish, should be encouraged to grow on and flower within a bed for seed saving.

Looking to Wild Crop Relatives for Resilient Resolutions

Many current commercial seed varieties will struggle with the changing climate, and some researchers are looking to the wild cousins of our food crops for adding potential resilience. Many of these wild relatives still grow naturally and have evolved to rough it out and survive in tough conditions. They may offer a new source of valuable genetic diversity that could be used to help futureproof those crops most at risk. The Crop Trust's Crop Wild Relatives Project is bringing together plant breeders, researchers, industry professionals, and farmers from around the world to try to boost climate resilience in our food chain. Over a period of 6 years, 100 scientists from 25 countries identified the wild relatives of 28 globally important crops. From apple and alfalfa to barley, bean, and banana, the aim is to help develop crops that withstand greater extremes of weather.

HOME PROPAGATION

Peach, Nectarine, Plum, and Apricot Trees

Stone fruit pits can be used to grow new trees that will be like the parent plant and thus are easier to work with. If you have existing trees that are growing well, try growing more by planting out some of their fruit stones. You can process the stone (and seed) in a more labor-intensive way, but directly planting stones outside at the end of the year replicates "letting nature take its course." This is what happens with fruit trees in the wild, and as we've discovered there is resilience to be found in trees that are able to adapt and flourish in tougher conditions, so don't pamper the seed. Try planting the stones out in a few places and see what emerges the following year.

If you don't have any of these fruit trees yourself, then see who does in your area. This is a great excuse for some barter and exchange. Only work with plump, healthy fruit that is disease-free and full of vitality and flavor.

Hard- and Softwood Cuttings

There are whole books on the topic of propagating fruit trees by taking cuttings, so I'm going to provide a few examples of some of the best produce with which to work, easily and resiliently.

- **Hardwood cuttings** are best taken in winter when the plant is dormant—examples include soft fruits such as black currants and gooseberry, figs, grapes, pomegranates, mulberries, and quince.

- **Softwood cuttings** are best taken in the summer and can be started from herbs such as rosemary, oregano, thyme, sage, and lavender.

Only choose to save from branches (and plants) that are healthy and disease-free. Take cuttings from the tips of branches (about a hand in length) from the new year's growth as they will have more energy to root. A diagonal cut is recommended using a sharp pair of pruners. Insert the base of the stem about 1 inch (2.5 cm) deep into a bare batch of ground and leave them alone. Come the following spring, you will see which have rooted and which have not.

To breed resilience, I am again working with the principle of natural selection, so this means no rooting hormone powder and no pampering to encourage them into life: just bare soil and the elements. The strongest will grow on through. These are the resilient plants you need for your garden right now. Prepare to be surprised by how many do grow on successfully with this light-touch approach. I've had black currant cuttings rooting from stems chucked into the compost heap.

Apples and Pears

Cuttings can be tried with pear trees, taken early in the year and placed into the ground. It's not quite as easy, so following the same principles as the other cuttings mentioned previously, try taking a few and experimenting.

← Black currant cuttings taking root in the ground

Apples can be grown from seed, but you don't know what you will end up with because apples trees are often grown on a grafted rootstock. If you have a lot of space, you can experiment with sowing seed. Apples do need diversity of varieties anyway in order to flourish, especially with all the challenges ahead. It's important to hedge your bets and even create an apple tree hedge of different varieties to see which ones fare best.

Wild varieties offer potential resilience, and mixed planting with other fruits is also key—see page 55 for more information about my own experiences. Grafting is a viable option for the creation of more resilient trees, but it is a little challenging to do. It involves taking a sliced cutting from a healthy tree and attaching (grafting it) onto resilient (normally dwarf) root stock.

Cuttings from Perennial Brassicas

Some of the best varieties of perennial brassicas include 'Nine Star' perennial broccoli, 'Purple Tree' collard, and 'Daubenton' and African kales. They will grow on reliably year after year. See page 74 for more information about the benefits of perennial vegetables.

To take cuttings, just remove a side shoot from the parent plant roughly a hand in length and use a pair of pruners to trim the bottom so it is a clean diagonal slice. Place

→ **FROM LEFT** Perennial kale cuttings

Avocado stones germinated in a compost pile—natural, easy propagation

your cuttings in some multipurpose growing medium in a large pot outside to give them the opportunity to grow.

Perennial Roots

Horseradish in a super-resilient plant. Once established it is hard to get rid of, and the root is incredibly good for you. I highly recommend growing it. See page 169 for more information on this amazing edible. Root cuttings are easy to do as this plant seriously wants to grow. Just dig down to the root and carefully work your way around it to remove a piece roughly 2 inches (5 cm) long, cut back the foliage (to conserve energy), and plant the root piece where you would like it to grow. A pot or another contained area might be a good place to start as horseradish will spread rapidly once established.

Rhubarb becomes crowded over time and needs to be dug up and divided (sliced into two or three pieces with a spade) every few years when the plant is dormant. This will provide you with extra plants to pass onto others, or to expand your own rhubarb patch.

Please see page 169 for more information on Jerusalem artichokes, oca, yacón, and other perennial crops.

7   Climate Change SOS

Quick solutions for extremes of weather, from floods and droughts to wildfires and insect plagues.

IN OUR VARIABLE, WHATEVER-THE-WEATHER FUTURE, acting quickly around changing conditions to reduce damage from extreme weather events is going to be key. Over time hopefully community infrastructures and defenses will be heightened to further reduce damage, but until then, knowing what to do in an emergency in the here and now is essential.

I know it's really difficult, but the more we experience these challenges, the more we will become well versed at adaptation and can, in turn, help others to prepare. We will cope, we will flourish, and we will work together for a better future for us all.

← Drought-inflicted ground

Wildfires Are Imminent

Around the world, intense periods of drought and heat have made wildfires an increasing, real, and wide-ranging threat. Not just confined to longsuffering areas, such as Southern Europe and California, recent years have seen wildfires rage across the globe in multiple, previously unaffected regions and at more ferocious levels overall. It's important for us all to know how to cope should a wildfire strike.

WHAT TO DO IN THE EVENT OF A WILDFIRE

- **Create a fire defense zone** about 30 feet (9 m) wide around your home or garden where no flammable materials are present. Remove any wooden or dry materials that could catch fire, including wooden benches, ladders, wheelbarrows, or dry wood or foliage. If you have tall shrubs or trees close to your home, try to cut them back or down if possible.

- **If you have an irrigation system, use it** on the outer perimeter of your property to keep the soil as moist as you can. Water the soil closer to your home by any means necessary as it can potentially help slow a blaze.

- **Ensure any compost heap is as moist as possible.** Dry compost heaps were the cause of wildfires in London and elsewhere in recent years.

- **A nearby wildfire also carries the risk** of polluted ash debris landing on your soil and plants. This ash can contain a lot of chemicals. Some people recommend using covers over your garden as a protection from this, but these materials can in themselves be flammable, so do consider your options here wisely. You might be better off physically removing ash from the ground and plant leaves afterwards.

WHAT TO DO WHEN STORM FORCE WINDS ARE FORECAST
- **Move lighter pots or hanging baskets** to a secure location (near or inside a home) so they are protected from being blown over and broken.

↓ **BELOW, FROM LEFT**
Strong winds can cause a lot of damage to the garden.

Securing plants against wind damage is essential if you live where high winds are prevalent.

- **Ensure that any tools and equipment,** such as wheelbarrows, are safely out of harm's way. Any lighter object can at best be picked up by gusts and blown away; at worst, the force of a gale can pick up and smash the object, causing damage to your home.

- **Taller plants and structures are more vulnerable** to wind damage than crops that are closer to the ground. Secure any tall crops by tying them securely to stakes and cages so they are more firmly rooted in the ground. Likewise, you might consider slightly cutting back some plants (e.g., climbing beans) if the foliage is sprawling as that will make it more vulnerable to wind.

- **Wind can have an extreme cooling impact** on plants that can further cause damage. There is safety in numbers, so to manage this threat move plant pots together close to your home or in corners to afford protection.

- **If wind damage has already occurred to plants,** add water and try applying a mulch to give them the opportunity to recover. You might also try cutting back any apparent damage to see if that helps the plant to conserve energy and continue growing.

I'M WORRIED MY GARDEN IS GOING TO FLOOD! WHAT CAN I DO?

- **Put out any large containers,** even bins or basins, to help collect water and try to stem the on-the-ground flow.

- **If you have rain barrels or a cistern** and they are currently full, try emptying them with a hose into the soil elsewhere in the garden. Think: slow it, spread it, sink it as much as you can.

- **Community action can make all the difference** when it comes to flood risk. If you have immediate neighbors also at risk, then maybe ask them to put empty containers outside to try to reduce the amount of runoff water.

KIM'S TIP

Savvy Idea

You also could dig an impromptu rill (rainwater channel) to help move water away from your vegetable garden if the situation and time allows. Think about where the water can be channeled to pass through because you don't want to cause someone else's garden space to flood in the process. Use piles of any mulch materials you might have, such as wood chips or compost, to form a natural flood barrier or berm. They also can help soak up some of the excess water to an extent, depending on the level of the flood risk pending.

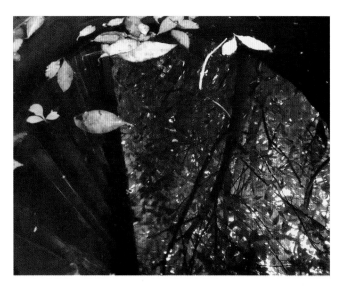

↑ **ABOVE, FROM LEFT**
Put out large containers to collect water to help slow the flow.

These houses are protected from river flood by way of a floodplain in the form of a river overflow.

- **If you have any outside electrical supply,** make sure it is turned off. Also remove electrical equipment.

- **If you have to leave gas-powered tools** where they are at risk of damage, empty their tanks to avoid floodwater contaminants.

- **Secure any fruit or vegetable cages** with extra supports to keep them from floating away.

- **Any sheds or outdoor structures** will need to be locked and defenses shored up. Consider using sandbags where possible to try to provide protection from floodwaters building up.

- **Pick up any pots, materials, and tools** that you can and move them safely out the way—garden furniture and composting supplies, too. If you have any containers or bags of chemicals or fertilizers, these definitely need to be moved away to prevent the risk of chemical pollution.

- **If your plot is harvest laden,** quickly pick what produce you can because floodwaters can contain pollutants (hopefully not your own) that will effectively ruin your crop.

MY GARDEN HAS FLOODED! WHAT DO I DO NOW?

Unfortunately, vegetable gardens saturated with floodwater will have many ruined crops, especially those that are in the ground (i.e., root crops). A few days of being underwater will kill plants directly, and the high risk of pollutants means that any surviving crops will likely have to be discarded.

- **Be careful when touching floodwater** as it can be contaminated. Wear robust footwear, such as waterproof boots. Avoid stepping directly on soil when possible as that will further cause compaction and damage.

- **To rescue surviving plants and trees,** you could try raking trenches to see if that helps the water to dissipate. Try channeling the water away as best you can. For example, make a hole in a bank or berm for the water to move through, then create a soakaway.

- **Fashion a makeshift siphon** using an old piece of hose to help pick up the water and move it elsewhere.

← Carrying vegetables through a flooded street after heavy monsoon rains in Lahore. Severe flooding in Pakistan has displaced 7.9 million people.

Prevention and Drought-Cure Thinking

Consider adding or expanding rainwater collection systems to help slow the flow of accumulated rainwater when it is in ample supply. You'll be able to put it to good use in the garden for the future.

After the water dissipates, the ground is going to be damaged as a result of flooding. There are many potential outcomes, but mature soil will leach nitrogen and lose structure. Adding lots of organic materials afterwards to help rebuild soil health will be key. From compost and mulches, to using green manures over winter, this will all help the soil life to recover and repair the damage.

Weeds poking through the soil will be a surefire sign of the beginning of recovery as natural systems start to repair and reproduce. Consider using raised beds on your plot moving forward to help lift plant roots out of harm's way in the future.

↓ **BELOW, FROM LEFT**
Ground cover and mulching will help prevent soil drying out so quickly during a drought.

Mixed planting and no-till gardening will also protect the soil.

Water deeply, then apply a mulch to help keep water in the soil.

THERE IS LIKELY TO BE ANOTHER DROUGHT THIS YEAR, SO HOW SHOULD I PREPARE MY VEGETABLE GARDEN?

- **Leave space between water-hungry plants** so they can establish deeper, wider root systems. This will help them become more resilient. Plant crops deeper in the ground for the same reason. Consider mixed planting systems as outlined in further detail on page 53.

- **Plant more edible perennials** and leave crops in the ground for longer to maximize harvests and pick-and-come-again opportunities, without disturbing the soil and disrupting its ability to hold and maintain water.

- **Ground cover will be key** to help protect soil from drying out quickly. Maximize available space and crop harvests by filling every available gap with plants such as herbs and lettuce. Use sprawling plants, such as nasturtium and winter squash, to cover the ground between crops.

- **Don't dig your soil when it is saturated**—protect it and the many microorganisms living within. This will help reduce water needs and boost natural ecosystems to the benefit of plant resilience.

- **Avoid chemical fertilizers** and other products always as they are damaging to soils. As well as destroying wildlife (in addition to the designated pest), they damage the soil and create less biodiverse, needier spaces that are definitely not resilient.

- **Maximize water harvesting opportunities** with water barrels or even a small pond.

- **Some plants will be more resilient than others,** but there are tricks that can help reduce watering needs whatever the crop. There is lots of advice on page 70 about this.

- **Make the best use of local resources** for mulching to help protect plants and reduce watering needs overall. There are lots of freely available materials that can be used.

- **Reduce the water you are giving plants** in advance of an anticipated drought. Too much watering creates plants with shallowing root structures, leaving them more vulnerable to extremes. Deeper watering and watering much less often encourages plants to extend deeper root systems and creates more natural resilience.

KIM'S TIP

How to Cope with a Heatwave in a Polytunnel or Greenhouse

A prolonged period of heat can quickly turn an under-cover structure into a raging plant incinerator if sufficient ventilation isn't provided. These glass and plastic structures heat up super quickly and, before you know it, conditions inside can become too hot for plants.

Preventative measures need to be taken in advance. From opening doors, windows, and vents all night long to using partial shade-making materials to cover the structure, there are measures you can take to help provide plants some respite from the glare of the summer sun. It all makes a difference. Avoiding bare soil and using lots of ground cover also greatly helps the plants growing inside.

↑ My polytunnels grow wild to protect soil and plants growing within from drying out.

MY GARDEN IS BLANKETED IN SNOW! WHAT DO I DO?

Cold weather, frost, and snow can serve a beneficial purpose for gardens and soil. Killing off pathogens, pests, and disease. Some plants even need a certain number of hours of cold weather (called chill hours) in order to flower the following year. Snow itself can afford protection and insulation for plants. However, when the snowfall is extremely heavy, there will be a number of risk factors at play.

- **Sanded and salted roads and path**s create a potential for some of that material to get into your beds and soil.

- **The sheer weight of heavy snow** can impact the structure of plant leaves and stems, sometimes causing irreparable damage or death.

- **The actual process of brushing snow** off plants can cause even more damage than the snow itself because branches and foliage that are frozen become brittle and therefore are more at risk of breakage.

↓ **BELOW, FROM TOP**
Light snow-covered wheelbarrow

Rosemary blanketed in snow at my home

- **As the snow melts** there can be further risk of subsequent flooding.

Light snow can be left in place. In the case of heavy snow, the sheer weight of it can create a challenge for plants and structures such as polytunnels. The key is to gently brush off snow by hand to avoid damaging brittle stems and leaves, then use some form of cover to help protect more vulnerable trees and plants. Ideally, you want to continue allowing light through to the plant. Materials such as garden fleece (a.k.a. row cover), plastic sheeting, or mesh will help provide protection until the snow melts.

If you have concerns that plants have been damaged, it is best to wait until spring arrives to assess the situation. Sometimes it's best to leave any damaged foliage in place as this in itself can provide protection until warmer weather arrives. At that time, the damaged plant parts can be removed and composted.

The biggest risk of snow comes in late spring when seedling planting is well underway. The sudden influx of cold can catch more vulnerable seedlings totally unaware. Providing some form of covering to protect them will be essential.

Some Key Pest and Disease Plagues

An increasing risk of pests and disease is one of the expected challenges with our changing climate. Pests are migrating, and new pests are moving in. There are more opportunities for breeding and for them to overwinter and live longer. The risk of pest damage overall is higher. For these and many other reasons, there is a whole chapter on working with wildlife for natural pest control later in this book. Boosting predator numbers will help immensely, and in that environment, it's much harder for one type of creature to get out of control and cause an extensive amount of damage. Disease also can spread more readily among plants that are weakened by extreme weather conditions.

← Aphids being hunted down by a ladybug

What do you do, though, if you walk outside one day and some of your plants are absolutely covered with pests? We commonly think of locust infestations when we use the phrase "insect plagues," and the desert locust is now the world's most devastating migratory pest. What will the future hold as pests—migratory and otherwise—take advantage of our heating planet?

We aren't talking a few critters that can just be safely picked off and removed. We are talking widespread, damaging levels of infestations that can occur when plants are at greater risk from extreme weather. What does a gardener do then? Here's a quick lowdown on longer-term, natural pest prevention for certain pests, along with a quicker cure for each.

HOT WEATHER–LOVING PESTS

These particular pests love causing mayhem when the thermostat rises as it creates more opportunities for them to multiply and chow down on heat-weakened plants that might otherwise be more resilient to such attack.

Aphids and Thrips

These insects are able to reproduce on their own, and they will do so with gusto in hot weather. They suck the juices out of plant stems and leaves and secrete a sticky residue that can lead to further issues with mold and plant damage and disease. Many of our pest patrol heroes, such as ladybugs and lacewings, love eating aphids, so the natural solutions outlined on page 133 will help longer term.

Quick-Fix Removal

Spray aphids off plants with a water hose spray. It also is possible to pick them off by hand. Sometimes you can remove a few particularly infested leaves to reduce numbers significantly. If your plant is in a pot inside, placing it outside for natural predators (if the weather allows) can be a brilliant natural solution.

Spider Mites

These insects will damage leaves as they feed off them, causing brown and yellow stippling on the foliage. Their population will surge if untested by natural pest control in hot conditions.

Quick-Fix Removal

Squash and remove spider mites from leaves and try to encourage natural pest control
as these pests can provide vital food for many creatures, from ladybugs and lacewings
to wasps, hover flies, predatory mites, and many other beneficials.

Cabbage White Butterfly Caterpillars (Cabbage Worm)

While the sight of butterflies on a warm sunny day is lovely to see, the off-white
butterflies that give birth to these wanton destroyers of brassica plants are another
matter entirely. A few can be brushed off by gardeners and resilient plants alike, but
drought-weakened brassicas, especially smaller seedlings, can be easily overcome. Perennial brassica and healthy leaves in a mixed planting system can mainly bounce back from
a nibble or two, but out of control numbers are a different matter entirely.

Quick-Fix Prevention and Removal

Picking off the caterpillars by hand is the fastest way of removing this threat when it has landed. Check the underside of leaves as the caterpillars tend to hide there. Consider netting some of your plants if you feel further protection is needed. In a mix-and-match planted bed, good companion plants such as rhubarb, nasturtium, garlic, feverfew, and onion can further lend a helpful, deterrent hand.

WET WEATHER–LOVING PESTS AND DISEASES

Slugs and Snails

These slippery suckers do not like hot weather at all. They can't easily breed or thrive in hot conditions. They need moist, shaded conditions to prosper and reproduce. Not all slugs are as much of a threat, and some species are actually less ferocious plant eaters and prefer eating material that is already breaking down, so they are in fact a useful ally in the compost pile.

→ My chickens are fed slugs on my homestead (although I don't watch).

Quick-Fix Prevention

If you have an issue with slugs, there are many things you can do. First, reduce their numbers by going out at dusk armed with a bucket and (if so inclined, a hunter's hat) and remove them by hand from your plot. How you do this depends on how you feel. I personally tend to place slugs in and around my chicken enclosure, but then I walk away and don't look. . . .

Second, if there is an issue with slugs in your patch, be extra careful when planting out seedlings as they are particularly vulnerable to attack. Hold off, pot them up, then plant them out as bigger seedlings with deeper roots that are stronger and therefore more resilient.

Place a plank of wood down on your beds and use this to tease out slugs for easy removal. They will hide in the moist conditions underneath. Also, try to think about where the slugs are coming from—raised beds can deteriorate over time and become breeding habitats for slugs, so do check. Beds too near to hedges and other dark undergrowth can be especially problematic.

Natural control measures include deterrents, such as eggshell and wool pellets, placed around plants. You can also use copper tape around pots and beer traps. There are many predators that can lend a helping hand, from birds and amphibians to spiders and ground beetles.

BLIGHT AND POWDERY MILDEW

Wet, warm weather will exacerbate the spread of certain troublesome airborne diseases. Powdery mildew is much less of a troublesome fungal concern than blight; its damage is normally fairly localized. Blight, on the other hand, can spread with abandon from leaf to leaf and plant to plant as the airborne spores take hold. Tomato plants and potato crops can become decimated in no time at all.

Quick-Fix Prevention

Adequate airflow and sufficient distancing between at-risk plants will help keep the condition in check. Remove leaves that are infected and allow space between leaves to help slow the flow of spores.

Water the plants on the ground, directed into soil itself. Seriously consider employing a system of mixed planting in future (see page 53) where plants from the same family are sufficiently distanced apart to reduce the risk of infection spreading.

8 Natural Pest Control in a Changing Climate

How to deal with introduced pests, encourage a diversity of "good bugs," and create a balance so pests don't become problematic in the first place.

← My biodiverse gardens are rich with wildlife and natural pest control.

GREATER RISK OF PEST AND DISEASE form one of the main threats of our changing climate. Extreme weather events can weaken plants. At the same time, warmer, wetter seasons can create conditions where new and existing pests proliferate, with potentially more breeding, overwintering, migratory opportunities overall. This means more pests and more weakened plants that may be more susceptible to attack.

Whichever way you look at it, natural predators are going to be an important ally. The more you can create a more balanced ecosystem with plenty of these natural helpers around, the better your garden will be. It will be much harder for one type of creature to get out of control and cause damage to your precious crops.

Wildlife, wildflowers, and even some weeds have a valuable role to play in a garden or allotment, creating a natural balance and valuable, diverse habitats where so-called pests can become food for something else. This doesn't mean you want your vegetable garden entirely overgrown or messy. Far from it. It's just that the natural world shouldn't be sidelined. It should be welcomed in with gusto to create a space that is attractive and truly healthy and teeming with life, vitality, and a natural resilient order.

Learn to Grow a Little Wild

For so many years there has been a perception that our vegetable gardens should be super tidy and that gardeners should meticulously remove any weed that dare appear, pick off all slightly discolored, damaged foliage, and possibly panic at the sight of bugs on the ground. Yet in doing so we are removing potential habitats and food for the beneficial wildlife that can help keep pest numbers in check.

→ A wild corner of a vegetable garden is filled with long grass, wildflowers, and a pile of dead wood. Nearby weeds (such as stinging nettles) are growing to boost biodiversity.

KIM'S TIP

Natural Pest Control: Ladybugs

The immature larvae of ladybugs/lady beetles are hungry and ready to hunt down aphids. They can eat hundreds and hundreds—thousands even—during their lifetime. They don't harm plants in any way, and they also eat other pests such as mealybugs and leafhoppers. Stinging nettles, fennel, dill, and chives are among the best plants to help draw these vegetable garden heroes your way.

← Ladybug larvae will hunt down aphids for you.

In a more climate change–savvy vegetable garden, all creatures have a role to play, and many often-maligned insects are either beneficial predators or useful in the food chain overall. And it's really not hard to welcome wildlife in. Maybe begin by allowing a few areas of grass to grow a little longer, creating a few corners where weeds will be allowed to move in. Or plant a few wildflowers in and around your vegetable garden where they'll provide a welcome splash of color in the process.

Ground cover is very important for wildlife, so why not create a leaf or wood pile somewhere, let some salad leaves or herbs spread out, mature, and flower? A wildlife pond is incredibly easy to create from salvaged materials, too.

Little by little, the natural world will be better able to lend a helping hand. The more you allow it, the more you will see and understand the bigger picture of synchronicity and satisfaction to be found therein. The sight of beetles, bugs, or butterflies fluttering on by; bees, wasps, and hover flies busy pollinating plants; and birds hectically but adorably flying overhead can't fail to bring happiness and hope for the future of us all.

MAKE YOUR GARDEN AN EAT-AND-BE-EATEN WORLD

In permaculture principles, a pest problem is as indication that predators are required to restore the balance. Although this idea of biodiversity and natural order isn't something that will immediately happen overnight, wildlife and nature will move in quickly if given half a chance.

Even small changes of habitat can reap big rewards. A resilient garden is one that is full of nature's little helpers, where every creature generally has its place, even if only as food for something else. A resilient garden is well and truly teeming with life, to the benefit of healthy, abundant produce, natural pest control, and the well-being of person, plate, and planet.

Such a nature-robust garden also is a much more enjoyable place than a garden that is high maintenance and needy of pest control products and our attention (fertilizers and weeding!). That kind of garden is much more vulnerable to pest attack in our changing climate.

The Longer-Lasting Damage of "Quick-Fix" Chemical Pest Control

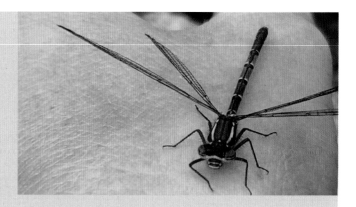

There is more awareness in recent years of the negative impact of pesticides on bee populations, yet the damage of these chemical interventions can be felt across the entire natural world. From earthworms, frogs, hover flies, beetles, and butterflies, many other creatures are negatively affected. This is the last thing the natural world needs when wildlife numbers are already struggling because of reduced habitat availability and climatic changes. Working closely with wildlife to grow better food and create a healthier ecosystem for our ailing planet is absolutely integral for all.

The range of pesticides commonly available to purchase from gardening outlets includes:

- Insecticides: products that kill insects
- Fungicides: products that target molds and fungi
- Herbicides: products that kill unwanted weeds

The manufacturers claim that the products are designed for a particular issue (e.g., to kill aphids), yet the truth of the matter is that the toxic impact reaches much further afield than that one targeted species.

↑ Protect wildlife, such as this damselfly, by gardening naturally.

← **FROM LEFT** Frogs love water and will move in readily if you have even a basic wildlife pond.

In a balanced garden, pests are not an issue. Let the natural world lend a helping hand for natural pest control.

A garden that is biodiverse, however, works in harmony with the natural world and there is a much greater hardiness as a result. The sight and sound of wildlife is delightful for you the gardener, and it takes being outside tending your low-maintenance space to a whole new level of enjoyment.

DAMAGE ON THE GROUND

As outlined in chapter 2, belowground resilience and soil ecology are absolutely key to a climate change–savvy vegetable garden. To help with water retention and absorption, to boost plant health and vitality, and to enable the natural ecology to come to the aid of our crops, our soils need to be alive and robust with microorganisms and wildlife. For drought, storms, or any other weather protection, our soils absolutely matter, and it is essential that we nurture, rather than damage, the beneficial soil web systems for the future.

INVASIVE PEST PROBLEMS

Since global trade routes opened wide with passengers, cargo, and flora and fauna being transported daily across the world, so the risk of invasive species snowballed. While many nonnative insects that are carried away in a tourist's bag or within a shipbound pallet will not survive the journey or changing climate, some can and will. When they manage to reproduce, settle, and spread, the on-the-ground impact starts becoming clear.

In addition, with changing climates, shifting seasons, and a general unbalance of life on Earth, some insects are "migrating" in ways we wouldn't have though possible before. New regions and climates are becoming attractive, and changing jet streams

↑ The Asian longhorn beetle

and weather patterns are fueling shifts in the geographic ranges of certain pests. This means new potential challenges to our fruit and vegetable growing are moving in fast.

The fire ant, Asian citrus psyllid, spotted lantern fly, and Japanese beetles in the United States are among the most recent interlopers. The damage and control of these and many other invasive species in America is estimated to cost $1.5 billion annually. The United States Department of Agriculture (USDA), which conducts ongoing research, estimates the real costs of the estimated 6,500 invasive plant, animal, microorganism, and pathogen interlopers actually comes in significantly higher. The Asian long-horn beetle, which has caused quarantines in four states at the time of this writing, would decimate the American forest industry if it were to spread.

Here in the United Kingdom., we have the Asian hornet, the oak pro-cessionary moth, the brown marmorated stink bug, and the harlequin ladybird, among many others. In the case of the harlequin, it was first introduced to mainland Europe to help control aphids before it made its way to the United Kingdom. It has been decimating the local

A Snapshot of a Chemical Catastrophe for a Garden Wildlife

Beyond perhaps lobbying for the implementation of more regenerative practices, we have little control over any chemicals used in our local parks or in the gardens and on the farms of others. But our gardens are our domain. Every organic, naturally worked garden, balcony, and homestead matters. We can all help do our bit.

What happens when wildlife is exposed to these products? Earthworms have increased mortality and decreased reproduction, possibly stunted growth and altered feeding habits, so these heroes of the soil are harmed. Bird populations already struggle and there is evidence of poisoning in tissues. Our feathered friends are also damaged when they eat pesticide-laden insects or earthworms or crop seed that has been coated with fungicides or pesticides.

ladybug population ever since, reducing its numbers by an estimated 44 percent. The same thing has happened in the United States, where this species also has been introduced.

With all of these and other pest challenges, boosting biodiversity of planting is essential. Mono-planted beds are simply more vulnerable to attack than free-planted (polyculture) mixed fruit and vegetable gardens. Biodiversity of wildlife is key because the more predators you have preying upon these insect pests, the more they can be further kept in check.

The Resilient Gardener's Guide to Helping and Not Hindering, Natural Pest Control

DON'T PANIC WHEN YOU SEE INSECTS

All too often people panic when they see a bug in their garden. With a preconceived idea that all bugs are bad bugs, we continually strive for a so-called picture-perfect, almost

← Make a judgment call on whether a so-called pest, such as this snail, is causing damage or not.

sanitized garden. The sight of bugs can cause alarm and panic in equal measure. Even if you do spot a pest, it doesn't necessarily mean game over for your plants.

SO HOW TO DO YOU KNOW IF A CREATURE IS FRIEND OR FOE?

If you just see one or two of a predetermined pest, be inclined to leave them be. If you see a lot of a pest and they are causing obvious damage, then it's time to act. Mixed planting helps enormously with natural pest control as it's simply so much harder for pests to find what they are looking to eat. For example, I never cover any of my plants to protect them from cabbage white butterflies because my brassica plants are so spread out, these pests never become much of an issue.

Here are a few examples of creatures that undeservedly have a bad reputation:

Wasps

These flying insects are actually very useful. I know they can be a pain at late-summer BBQs buzzing around your food, yet in the weeks before, they have been diligently working away, helping to pollinate your plants, eating the aphids off your broad beans and the caterpillars from your cabbages, and being incredibly beneficial all round. They get aggressive later in the year because they are starting to die off with the arrival of fall's cooler temperatures, so it's fair to forgive and ignore this in light of their overall helpfulness.

↓ Wasps also are useful pollinators and predators.

Ants

Ants have a bad reputation and are seen as something to be removed, poisoned at worst or moved away at best. Why is this? Yes, they do farm aphids for their sweet honeydew milk, but this doesn't mean that having ants near your plants is going to cause an explosion of aphids. I have lots of ants living in my poly-tunnels and have never found them to be an issue. They help pollinate plants and generally help to clear up debris and take it away to use in their colonies below ground. Plus, I think there are many more as yet unknown benefits of ants besides.

Sure, if their anthill is right by a plant's roots, that might cause an issue, but I've never experienced that myself. If I think there are too many ants in a colony, then once or twice I have moved them

Do I Need to Do Something about This Potential Pest?

To decide if something needs to be done about an insect—or whether said insect can just be left be—start by taking some time to look and learn from whatever insects you see in your garden. This may seem obvious, but you can learn a lot just by paying close attention.

- What is the creature doing?
- Is it visibly damaging your plants?
- Are there a lot of said potential pests?
- Is this something that needs to be dealt with now? Can you leave them a day or so to see what happens?
- Could this insect be beneficial in some way useful (e.g., a predator itself)?
- Are its numbers so low that arguably it could be left?

Let common sense prevail. A bed filled with slugs or a plant covered from top to bottom with aphids is in trouble and will require urgent intervention. But a plant with a slight nibble or a few aphids doesn't require any action because the natural predators will likely step in to help.

In a balanced garden, pests aren't typically an issue. Yes, a leaf may have a hole or two, but it's worth waiting and watching to see what happens. As the biodiversity of your outside space builds, the opportunities for natural intervention will grow with each passing year.

To give you an example, I have turned purple spouting broccoli semi-perennial in my polytunnels, as it can in fact grow on for many years (up to seven under cover) (see page 158 for more information on how to do this). One spring my plants became covered in aphids. I have not had an issue with aphids in the polytunnels, so this was a new experience. It became apparent that the plants had been weakened by the previous summer's heatwave and drought, and they had become more vulnerable to attack as a result. I watched and waited for a week, deliberating what to do before the aphid numbers became a more significant issue. Then, before I was about to jump in, I spotted an unusual looking interloper on some salad leaves nearby, then another and another, and then I spied ladybug larvae in more advanced stages of development and knew what was happening. They were coming to the aid of the brassica. I had never seen so many aphids before, but equally, I had never seen so many ladybug larvae. Soon the natural order was miraculously restored.

Slug Prevention Tips

A few slugs are fine because they help break down decaying organic matter. Too many though and plants will be damaged. So, while you wait for biodiversity (i.e., your army of amphibian slug eaters) to build and help keep slug populations down, there are measures you can take to help keep numbers in check.

- If slugs are turning up more than you'd like, work out where your slugs are living/coming from so you can outwit them and make a dent in their numbers. Check that your raised beds aren't rotting. Over time as they age, the wood can start to deteriorate and become a home for slugs. In this instance, your lovely beds can transform into a slug breeding factory.

- Before planting out in a bed, lay down a wooden plank or two in the area first. If there are slugs present, they will shelter underneath this plank in the daytime, making it easy to remove them prior to planting the bed.

- Only plant out healthy, robust seedlings as they will be better able to handle a little nibble or two. The bigger the seedling, the better, because they will be stronger and less liable to be destroyed overnight.

- Patrol your plot. Seedlings are most vulnerable, so have a look at dusk over the first night or two. This is when the slippery suckers are most likely to emerge and wreak havoc.

- Get a pond. Look to build your collection of slug eaters by encouraging amphibians, birds, ground beetles, and small garden snakes by installing a pond. If you can entice them in, they will all do their bit, helping to keep slug numbers in check.

- Try to avoid planting too close to hedges or areas in which slugs might be hiding.

↑ A plank of wood laid on the ground will attract slugs for easy hand removal.

on. The benefits of their presence far outweigh the negative, and I will only intervene if they get a little too populous for my plot. It's a different story if you garden where fire ants are present, as they do have a painful bite and aggressive nature.

Earwigs

These rather unattractive-looking creatures are brilliant fast-moving predators, and they are to be encouraged. Yes, they might have a slight nibble on your lettuce or sweet corn if it is left in the ground for too long, but their benefits far outweigh any negatives. They are a useful ally.

The Top Ways to Attract and Support Beneficial Wildlife

WEAVE IN ATTRACTIVE HABITATS

Longer grass and a biodiverse range of wildflowers and other plants help provide food and ground cover for many useful creatures. Even small corners of your garden used in this way can make all the difference.

The wild grasses around my fruit trees and soft fruits at the back of my vegetable patch also work as a protection against flooding because they soak up more water.

Piles of leaves, twigs, and upturned empty pots also afford valuable wildlife shelter, as will a compost pile over winter. A wildlife pond provides a source of liquid refreshment and an attractive habitat for everything from amphibians, birds, dragonflies, and bats.

ALLOW SOME WEEDS TO GROW

Although you don't want these wilder plants to take over your garden completely, having some weeds weaved in with existing plantings can provide many natural benefits during summer and over winter as ground cover to protect soil.

↑ **ABOVE, FROM TOP**
An earwig hunting in a tomatillo flower head

You don't need a dedicated bug hotel, but they can be fun to make with materials you have to hand.

↑ Allow some stinging nettles to grow.

The greater the variety of plantings you have, the more opportunities there are likely to be for wildlife to proliferate. Certainly in the case of bees, having plants that flower as much of the year as possible, and at different times, is incredibly useful.

Dandelions

Allow some to flower in your lawn early (and late) in the year. They provide a valuable source of food for pollinators when little else is available. They also help draw in many beneficial creatures, such as hover fly whose larvae are fantastic garden predators.

Stinging Nettles

These plucky weeds provide an incredibly valuable habitat for beneficial predators, such as ladybugs and lacewings. I even allow some to grow in my polytunnels to help ensure I have a supply of these garden heroes at my disposal in the growing season.

Queen Anne's Lace

This ancestor of the carrot grows readily in the wild and is much beloved by many insects, bees, wasps, and flies. It is listed as a noxious weed in some states in the United States, and it is very similar in appearance to poison hemlock, another member of the carrot family you definitely don't want to be growing, so just be aware. If permitted, it would grow well in wilder areas of your resilient garden space.

Phacelia

This pretty plant can be grown to attract an array of wildlife. From beetles and butterflies to lacewings, hover flies, and bees, it is a brilliant ally for natural pest control. In addition to this, the blooms make lovely cut flowers and the crop itself can be used as a green manure. See page 197 for more on using green manures.

BUILD A WILDLIFE POND

Adding a pond is one of the best actions you can take to encourage hungry pest-eating amphibians into your outside space. It benefits many other creatures to boot, including birds, dragonflies, and small mammals.

You don't need an elaborate construction or expense. Quite the opposite in fact. A pond can easily be made out of materials you happen to have to hand: It could be an old sink or wash basin buried into the ground so its rim is flush to the surface surrounding. Add some stones or bricks so creatures can get out as well as in to drink water and use the space. You need to ensure that wildlife won't get trapped inside and drown.

Groundcover plants surrounding your pond are useful. Amphibians especially benefit from having protection from predators or from the glare of the summer sun. Even the simplest of structures can be used to create a viable wildlife pond, and within no time at all the natural world will make use of this space and move right on in.

↓ Even a small pond can make all the difference and draw wildlife in.

NATURAL PEST CONTROL IN A CHANGING CLIMATE

→ **FROM LEFT**
Encourage wildlife with gusto.

Seed heads over winter for birds and bugs

Chamomile makes a good groundcover plant.

FEED THE BIRDS

Our feathered friends are a delight to behold fluttering back and forth with their excitable chatter. During the pandemic, especially over winter when there wasn't much gardening outside to be had, so many people benefited from the mesmerizing sight of garden birds frequenting bird feeders near the home. I heard of elderly care homes or people who were completely housebound attaching feeders to windows so residents could enjoy the display up close.

Garden birds also have a vital role to play in biodiversity and for natural pest control in your garden. Invite them in with gusto. Bird feeders during the winter months are key. Don't forget a water source of some form as well, even a plate or bowl with water in will suffice.

Leaving seed heads on plants over winter is a valuable source of food and shelter for many creatures. Likewise, allowing some leaf litter and not cleaning up the vegetable patch at the end of the growing season provides cover for the insects that make up an important part of the winter foraging for birds.

Garden birds will work hard on your behalf, during the summer months, pecking off pests such as caterpillars and slugs. Welcome them and help them stay around to the benefit and well-being of all.

GROUNDCOVER PLANTING

Bare soil isn't great at any time of the year. It leaves the soil more vulnerable to erosion over winter and drying out during the summer. Having some plants covering the soil helps a great deal. During the summer months, making use of any raised beds or growing areas is very sensible anyway and it helps create an attractive habitat for wilder biodiversity.

Some of the best filler plants for ground cover around crops include:

- **Nasturtium:** the leaves and flowers are lovely in salads
- **Calendula:** great for pollinators and has many edible and medicinal uses
- **Mixed salad leaves**
- **Summer herbs,** such as parsley, basil, and cilantro/coriander
- **Rocket/arugula:** also a good ground cover around taller crops

ALLOW PLANTS TO COMPLETE THEIR NATURAL CYCLE

Rather than pulling plants out when they have finished producing, or have bolted and started to flower (e.g., rocket, radish, or cilantro/coriander), leave them in the ground to continue flowering. The edible blooms are great for wildlife and biodiversity and can

→ Allow some plants, such as the brassica pictured, to grow on and flower for pollinators and other beneficial creatures.

be used as edible flowers in the kitchen, or indeed for cut flowers to bring to the table. I use a lot of vegetable patch flowers for decoration. They are so much better than the chemical-coated supermarket cut flowers. They are no-cost, require zero food miles, and are great for wildlife. What's not to like?

Extra Groundcover Planting Ideas for Enhanced Pest Predation

Cilantro/coriander is very attractive to lots of natural pest predators, such as lacewings, hover flies, and parasitoid wasps.

Feverfew has a smell that is considered a deterrent for some pests. It is also very attractive to hover flies so it helps draw these beneficial predators and pollinators in.

→ Feverfew works well by luring in beneficial insects for natural pest control.

Natural Pest Patrol

Lacewings

As with ladybugs, it is the immature larvae that are the most enthusiastic predators, hunting down aphids, mites, and other small insects with gusto. To draw these hugely beneficial creatures in, grow plants such as fennel, cilantro/coriander, and dill.

Hoverflies

These beautiful predatory flies are hungry for aphids when they are larvae and will provide a valiant natural pest control function by chowing down on mealybugs, aphids, and many other pesky critters. Popular plant attracters include dill, yarrow, feverfew, fennel, lemon balm, and parsley flowers.

Parasitic wasps

How they help keep pest numbers in check is a little akin to a scene from a low-budget horror film: The pest ends up worse for wear, or rather, eaten alive from eggs laid on or inside it by your friendly neighborhood parasitic wasp.

Plants that help attract these natural predators include dill, feverfew, cilantro/coriander, fennel, English lavender, lemon balm, and parsley. In addition, they will help widen your natural pest patrol by attracting parasitic caterpillar-controlling braconid, ichneumonid, and Trichogramma wasps to the party.

↑ Lacewing larvae are brilliant predators.

9 Vegetable Garden Planting Guide

A crop-by-crop look at how to build resilience into your favorite edible garden crops—plus meet some untraditional crops that already come with resilience built in.

THERE HAS BEEN MUCH DEBATE over which crops and varieties will fare well in our changing climate and which ones will struggle the most. There are many factors at play: the growing climate you live in, the weather patterns and particular climatic challenges present that year, and the level of resilience built into your outside space. It's also about you, the gardener, as custodian of your plot: how well you are able to work around the changing weatherscape; how you and your garden grow together with the natural world to shore up the defenses; and how you foster the resilience and know-how that enables you to foresee issues, think on your feet, and outwit challenges as they emerge.

Here are some savvy solutions to help boost results vegetable by vegetable on your plot.

Less Planting, More Picking

Part of the problem with so-called modern methods of gardening—or gardening as we have been taught in recent times—is that there is this almost a fast-food mentality to growing. Sow a seed, grow the plant, reap, and pull, to be replaced with another, then another. It's a production-line approach.

Yes, you want to make the best use of the space you have available. Yes, you want to have healthy, productive harvests. But many plants can keep on giving for longer if we'll just allow them the opportunity to do so. Working in this longer-lasting, nature-friendly

← Harvest more for less work.

← Tomato plants and 'Crystal Lemon' cucumber trail on the ground, and over the edge of a raised bed, allowing the cucumber vine to root freely and grow wild.

way reduces the amount of planting and tidying up required, saves money, boosts soil resilience, and provides more produce per plant for longer. Seriously, what's not to like?

It is increasingly common knowledge that perennials are a most beneficial addition to the climate change–savvy vegetable garden (more on those resilient allies in a bit). Yet, some of this perennial power can be found in other traditional crops if they are just given the opportunity to grow on and offer value a bit longer. You only have to look at the extended root systems of such longer-lasting plants to see how nature can step in to lend a helping hand. Stronger, more robust stems, and hopefully some mycorrhizal fungi that is much better for the surrounding soil and its structure overall.

PRIME PLANT PICKS

Here's my pick of the easiest plants to grow for longer periods of time, which I have learned from just playing around over the years. I live in a tricky climate, high up in Wales in the United Kingdom, so there are bound to be more I haven't yet discovered or that don't work for me but might work for you. Experiment and push the boundaries of what is traditionally considered possible.

Broad or Fava Beans

Though they are not winter hardy in cold climates, in mild growing zones, it's such a delight in spring when these autumn-planted beans surge into production that bit earlier than more frost-tender varieties such as bush, pole, or runner bean. Especially delicious eaten before the pods get too large, smaller beans are popular with the French (and my household) eaten raw for crunchy salads. The more you pick, the more you get, and the smaller to medium-sized beans have a standout flavor over their larger, more beefy counterparts.

Once you have harvested all available beans, if you cut the plant back to around the height of a hand, in healthy soil it can keep on growing and dutifully produce another smaller, but still worthwhile, harvest in return.

↓ **BELOW, FROM LEFT**
Less planting and lots of picking naturally

Cut back your broad or fava bean plant after harvest for further production.

VEGETABLE GARDEN PLANTING GUIDE

↑ **ABOVE, FROM LEFT**
Leave smaller beets in the ground for lots of leaf picking opportunities the following spring.

Luscious pick-and-come-again salad leaves being harvested

Get more and bigger potatoes per plant.

Beets

In the plant's second year, this biannual will attempt to flower and set seed. Yet, leaving a few roots in the ground over winter and into spring will afford you with a bumper harvest of delicious spinach-like leaves early in the season. This trick helps during the hungry gap period of spring when not much else is available to harvest. The larger beet leaves are delicious cooked and the smaller, baby leaves work well in salad. The root itself will turn woody, but the wide supply of leaves it produces makes it worthwhile to let it stay in the vegetable patch.

Pick-and-Come-Again Salad Leaves

Loose-leaf varieties of lettuce work better as pick-and-come-again choices as there is sufficient airflow between leaves to prevent mildew from moving in and to better avoid the slugs that hide so easily within. The more you pick, the more you keep harvesting, a fine excuse if ever I heard one for more, and more, and more . . . delicious homegrown salads, fresh from your plot, window box, or allotment to your plate.

This nifty approach also works well with arugula/rocket and with herbs such as basil and cilantro/coriander. These three will all attempt to complete their natural cycle and flower (bolt), especially during dryer conditions, so the more you can keep new leaf growth occurring by picking and eating, the more harvest you'll reap in return.

Savvy Tip: Cilantro/coriander, basil, and rocket/arugula can be harvested after they have started to flower. Cut them back down to ground, above some new growth on the stem. The flowers themselves are delightful and can be eaten. I use them for decoration on meals to impress and in salads, just because I can.

Potatoes

When you harvest potatoes the normal way—by pulling the entire plant and its many tubers out of the ground at once—you invariably find a few teeny potatoes within. These haven't matured to a decent-size spud. So, rather than pulling the plant out whole, dig gently by hand around the outside of the plant to remove the larger potatoes, leaving the plant in situ and enabling it to push growth into the smaller, remaining tubers for further harvests.

BOUNTIFUL BRASSICAS

I've arguably saved the best for last . . . I found that some brassicas (chard and purple sprouting broccoli especially) can in fact be turned semi-perennial and kept in the ground for a number of seasons. You also can do this with flat-leaf kale. Like many of the best gardening experiences, this technique came about through sheer accident and experimentation.

← Some of your brassicas, such as purple sprouting broccoli, can be grown on for a number of years for bigger, more resilient plants.

Purple Sprouting Broccoli

Keep harvesting your spears and you will find, after a few flushes, that they start to look smaller and maybe the plant leaves begin to turn a little yellow. At this point, your purple sprouting broccoli will try to flower to set seed. This is a sign that the plant has produced enough and it's time to enable it to conserve its energy to keep growing for longer by cutting back. I allow some flowers to form as they are excellent for pollinators early in the season, but will otherwise cut the plant back. I allow some new growth above each cut-back stem. Be careful not to cut back too much because the plant needs to keep a few leaves to be given the opportunity to keep photosynthesizing.

Allowing airflow is important to help avoid rot over winter. Otherwise, left in situ, the plant will carry on and on. A nice mulch of compost in spring and maybe again later in the season is useful, as is planting legumes (peas and beans) nearby as they will fix nitrogen in the ground which your brassicas will love. Just one purple sprouting broccoli plant alone is akin to four-plants-in-one in terms of harvesting potential.

Chard works in the same way except with edible leaves. I have chard plants that are eight years old growing in the polytunnels. Outside they will last for at least a few years, especially if you afford them a little protection against the excess of winter rain.

HAPPINESS IN HERBS

If you were to just grow one thing—let it be herbs! . . . I can't emphasize enough how these flavor-packed plants are integral to the climate change–resilient vegetable garden, for biodiversity of wildlife and natural pest control. Herbs also do so much for you, the gardener—to have so many fantastic healthy flavors at your disposal to bring joy to mealtimes. And herbs are useful for ground cover around other plants to help with soil water retention, and for the sight, smell, and overall health of your vegetable garden.

Parsley

This vitamin C–laden hero can be tricky to germinate from seed, so try to save some of your own seed from plants in their second year, when as a biennial, they will flower and set seed. This will help create locally adapted, lower maintenance seedlings with plenty to spare.

Really wet soil can cause fungal and mold issues, and drought can cause yellowing of leaves, so boosting your soil's resilience as outlined in chapter 2 will be key to growing a resilient parsley crop. Also keep picking all year round to maintain airflow between leaves.

Chives

This flavor-packed plant is super-resilient and will grow back year after year in your garden. Just watch that it doesn't take over as it will self-seed with abandon and spread if given half the chance. I always have many chives plants self-seeding in the gravel each year, providing me with lots of baby plants to share. The fact that the seedlings are able to germinate and grow in gravel speaks multitudes about the hardiness of this herb.

Cut chives back regularly and eat the leaves to encourage new growth if leek rust (yellow spots) starts showing. This also allows greater airflow between the stems. Watch out for slugs also as they can hide at the base of this plant.

If necessary, grow chives where they won't cause a reseeding issue. I have some plants mixed into beds and in a dedicated gravel herb garden where they cannot spread. As well as enjoying multiple stem pickings, I grow chives for their punky, purple flower heads, which attract pollinators and make brilliant cut flowers.

↑ Chives will grow back year after year.

Basil

Reputed to be good grown next to tomatoes, I am more inclined to say grow it in gaps wherever you can so you have plenty to harvest for summer dishes. This maximizes the chances of success and reduces pest and disease risk.

Basil plants are rather sensitive to cold and heat, so planting in and around other plants will help either way. During summer months you can boost supplies by taking stem cuttings, removing the lower leaves, and placing the cuttings in a glass of water on a sunny windowsill inside to create further seedlings for free. Cover plants with a cloche earlier and later in the season to protect against frost risk.

Oregano and Marjoram

Commonly mistaken for each other, oregano is the hardier of the two and can grow back year after year, whereas marjoram will grow for a few years in mild climates but struggles more so in cooler Northern climates. I grow both in gravel beds. This helps to replicate the Mediterranean soil they evolved in and reduces necessary care and attention. It also helps reduce the risk of fungal rot, which can be an issue for both in damp soils. Airflow is key. Open up the plant by pruning to improve air movement. Both are also excellent for wildlife.

Rosemary, Sage, Thyme, and Lavender

These perennial Mediterranean herbs love sunny growing conditions, but they can stand firm over winter if soil is protected from becoming saturated. My gravel beds again afford perfect protection all year round for these beneficial herbs, even in the wet winters we get in Wales. Regular harvesting helps keep any fungal issues at bay, especially by removing lower leaves over winter to improve airflow and conserve the plant's energy for the following season.

Cut plants back by at least half of their height and width if they start looking sickly, with discolored leaves or dieback, to help them grow on. Also take cuttings to root if your plants become too overgrown and woody.

Mint

There are so many varieties of mint, and it has so many uses. It is another resilient hero, and it will take over with zesty abandon. I have lots of mint growing in the wilder areas of my gardens, and it spreads across wood chip mulch and gravel pathways—that provides me with lots of cuttings and plants to use for courses and to give away. I keep it firmly contained in my dedicated gravel herb garden where it sits with pride-of-contained-place by the polytunnels.

All mints are useful, but Korean mint is worth an extra look as it is especially attractive to bees and other beneficial wildlife. I find mint grows best in wild corners where it is free to find its own way, unaided by us.

↓ **BELOW, FROM LEFT**
Thyme is a resilient garden ally.

Mint is a lovely resilient hero, but it spreads vigorously, so be sure to grow it in a contained area.

Cilantro (Coriander) and a Canny Alternative

The lovely fragrant flavor of cilantro/coriander is a welcome addition to the kitchen. It can be grown under cover over winter and indeed all year round if protected from the cold. During hot weather it has a tendency to bolt (flower and set seed), so it's arguably better to work with earlier and later in the season. For summer pickings, I favor Vietnamese cilantro/coriander as it stands firm in hot weather and doesn't try to flower. It does need extra protection from drought, though, but a deep water and mulch generally work wonders.

Lemon Balm and Lemon Verbena

Pests seem generally put off by these lovely herbs, so the only main threat is the risk of overwatering and soggy conditions. Again, I grow these plants with a gravel mulch to help provide all-weather protection. The leaves of both of these lemon-scented herbs make a most delicious, calming, and reputedly healing tea.

Bulb Fennel and Bronze Fennel

Both will grow back year after year potentially. In the case of bronze fennel, it will grow anywhere. Bulb fennel will return if grown under cover and regularly harvested. The major challenge with bulb fennel is bolting during a drought. Some shade and mulching of the soil will help bulbs develop and reduce this risk. Also, cutting back fronds and layering them around the plant as an impromptu mulch can help.

PERENNIAL CROPS FOR THE WIN

Perennials are an obvious climate change–savvy vegetable garden choice, because they are much better able to handle a nibble or two and fight off pests, disease, and seriously erratic weather. And they can be much more self-sufficient; their watering requirements tend to be much lower because they can seek out water and nutrients from further afield. They do so through their deeper, more sprawling root systems and because they can form longer-lasting mycorrhizal relationships below ground. See page 154 for more information on how this works and the many benefits.

What's not to like about plants that keep on giving year after year? As well as being naturally hardier against extremes of weather and threat of pests or disease than annuals,

↑ **ABOVE, FROM TOP**
Cilantro/coriander will bolt during the summer but harvesting helps, although leaving some to flower is great for wildlife.

Vietnamese cilantro/coriander comes into its own during the summer, and unlike standard varieties, it doesn't bolt.

VEGETABLE GARDEN PLANTING GUIDE

→ **OPPOSITE** Growing fruit bushes will benefit your garden and provide lovely fruity harvests.

having some perennials on your plot will help soak up an excess of water to the benefit of the surrounding plants and your soil, especially over winter.

My gardens flooded—and I mean really flooded—a number of years back, so to lend more protection, I planted a lot of fruit trees and soft fruit bushes at the back of the garden as a first line of defense. This technique of a protective layer is known as a swale, and it has been used by different cultures for a long time. Perennial planting is an important part of the mixed planting in a swale because the deeper root structures of such plants bind the soil together, improve its structure, and enable your garden to better cope with an excess of water.

At the back of my gardens, I also have long grass and plants such as willow growing so there is a multilayered perennial defense. Further to this, perennials help nurture soil biodiversity and keep carbon in the ground due to the undisturbed nature of the soil surrounding these low-maintenance plantings.

Fruit Bushes

Black currant and gooseberry are especially robust, and they can easily be grown from bare-root or potted plants. They will start producing very quickly, within their second year. They also are easy to propagate from cuttings—see page 116 for more advice on how to do so.

Other resilient edible varieties of fruiting bushes to consider include blackberry, raspberry, and loganberry. All of these are rather rampant growers; grow them in an area

KIM'S TIP

Top Tips

Black currants are packed full of vitamin C and are very good for you. I always freeze a lot at harvest time so I can enjoy them throughout the winter months. Just place them loose on a tray in your freezer; when they have frozen solid, store them in an airtight container to pack into the deep freeze until winter.

Free mulches such as coffee grounds work well around acid-loving blueberries. Gooseberries benefit from the liming effect of small amounts of wood ash, if you have a fire.

Resilient Thinking

Some of the best drought-resilient varieties of fruit trees (once established) to consider growing are fig, apple, damson plum, guava, Asian pears, and loquat (Japanese medlar). Also consider wild varieties, such as wild cherry and wild apple.

where they won't take over. Blueberries are a lovely versatile fruit. They do require acidic soil; mulch them well with ericaceous compost or pine or conifer tree foliage.

Grape vines are a reliable fruiter, especially with warming summers. Their roots grow far and spread wide, resulting in a drought-tolerant nature. I have to grow mine indoors in a polytunnel at the moment, but that is likely to change in the near future. Cut the plant back heavily to its stem after fruiting to enable the plant to grow on and mulch well. Take cuttings over the winter to expand your fruiting supply.

FRUIT TREES

There is much uncertainty over which varieties of tree fruit will do well in which areas for the future. Before I get into the resilient growing tricks, let me just say that having a diversity of trees really helps. Native, wild varieties also are worth a look. See what is growing well elsewhere in your neighborhood. There will undoubtedly be issues in the future over the number of chill hours available and how much chill different varieties need. Plus, there will always be the risk of late frost for early-blooming trees, along with challenges from pests, diseases, and other factors. See page 53 for further tips around coping with different extremes. Until then here are some generic savvy tips and suggestions for fruit trees and bushes in general.

↓ Wild cherry tree fruit

Mix Plants and Layer

The more varieties you have, the better the chances of success. There also is protection and safety in numbers. For example, more vulnerable or young trees can be afforded protection by other, more resilient, fast-growing trees located nearby. Mixing and layering plants makes for a more resilient garden overall, as a barrier to strong winds, a source of partial shade during extreme heat, and protection from pests and disease because it's harder for them to spread. Just be sure to check the pollination requirements within your planting selection to make sure you have pollination partners available if needed.

Boost Soil Ecology

As we saw in chapter 2, microorganisms in the soil can help boost resilience, and plants and trees will benefit from symbiotic relationships with the mycorrhizal fungi in the soil. It will further encourage whatever-the-weather resilience.

Mulching and Soil Structure

Soil is your vital ally for futureproofing protection. Go no-till, boost fertility with compost, and mulch around the base of fruit trees (not touching the trunk) to improve water retention and absorption properties. Also consider using biochar to further create an attractive habitat for microbial activity within the ground.

Rhubarb

This fantastic perennial stalwart has a lot of edible uses, so it is rather exciting to grow. There's more to this plant than rhubarb crumble, that's for sure. Plants tend to struggle more when their roots have become compacted, which basically means they just need

Good Rhubarb Companions

Not all plants work well with rhubarb, but mixed plantings in between and around rhubarb plants maximizes space and keeps soil in the ground. Choose from the following:

- **Peas and beans:** Their nitrogen-fixing nature will aid the rhubarb longer term and create some shade protection from heat. These legumes also benefit from the aphid-deterring oxalic acid content of the rhubarb leaves.

- **Brassicas:** A few of these plants (kale and broccoli) work well and benefit from being near the pest-deterring content of the rhubarb leaves (whitefly and cabbage white butterfly, in particular).

- **Garlic:** These bulbs help cleanse the soil, so they are a great to help fend off weevil attacks for the rhubarb growing nearby.

Rhubarb leaves are fine to compost and can be used as an on-the-ground mulch around brassica plants.

more space in which to further spread their roots and grow. This happens roughly four or five years after being first planted.

To divide a rhubarb plant, dig up the root ball—basically the whole plant, ideally with roots intact. Using a sharp spade, divide it into three or four sections for replanting. This all needs to be done when the plant is in dormancy in winter or very early spring; it's a great way of getting more plants for your plot. Otherwise, these plants are highly resilient, requiring nothing more than a mulch of compost in the spring when you add compost elsewhere.

Asparagus

This most delicious vegetable is expensive to buy, and it is always best eaten fresh as the sugars start to convert to starch from the moment it is picked. Asparagus that has sat on a shop shelf for days is never going to compare to freshly picked and eaten spears. It's also not hard to grow. There are just a few considerations to ensure a healthy, resilient asparagus patch. Get this right, and you can be picking your own spears for twenty years to come.

Starting from crowns is easier than starting from seeds as you have to wait a few years before you can harvest your first spears. The crowns need time to establish, so

→ The excitement of
asparagus emerging

Savvy Tips for Asparagus Resilience

- **To boost their productivity,** give them seaweed if you can—either powder or fresh seaweed if you live near a beach.

- **When harvesting asparagus,** be careful to use a knife to slice the spear just beneath the surface. If you pull, you can damage the root below.

- **At the end of the asparagus-picking season—** which lasts just six to eight weeks in the spring—the remaining spears will shoot high and go to seed. Let them do this as the foliage it produces photosynthesizes and provides food to strengthen roots until they grow following year. Leave the stalks in the ground until spring (unless you have an asparagus beetle issue) when it is safe to remove them with the promise of more lovely spring spears to dutifully emerge from the ground in the weeks ahead.

- **Give your patch a thick mulch of compost** or manure in autumn. Give it an application of half-rotten leaf mold in spring to help keep weeds away and the keep the ground nice and moist and warmed for asparagus to emerge through.

- **Risk of damage by asparagus beetle** can be kept under control by removing spent asparagus foliage once it has died back in early winter. Haul it away from your patch because if you had an issue with this pest, then the spent foliage could still contain a few of them. Otherwise, remove any beetles and eggs by hand as you see them and boost natural pest control as much as possible. The odd beetle isn't going to cause too much of a problem, but their numbers need to be in balance.

- **Keep crowns fed and moist.** Mulching and boosting soil structure and moisture absorption and retention properties is a good idea.

growing from crowns provides you with a harvest quicker and means the plants are more likely to establish.

Asparagus needs its own competition-free patch: Getting the plants established is key. Choose a sunny spot with compost-rich, weed-free soil and plant your crowns in spring. Leave around 2 feet (61 cm) between plants and ensure the area they are in is kept free of weeds and other plants. Otherwise, interlopers will compete for nutrients and that impacts your plants' ability to get established, thrive, and produce.

→ Oca makes a great groundcover plant.

Oca

This tuber is increasing in popularity, and it's well worth a look. It's relatively small in size but delicious in taste, with pink and white, new potato–sized tubers produced below ground. Oca tubers have a lovely, almost slightly fruity, flavor. They can be cooked whole and added to a range of dishes.

Plant tubers in the spring in a sunny spot, then wait until the end of the growing season in mid to late autumn before the first frosts to harvest the roots. They do need a long period of growth, so leave them as long as you can before harvesting. The plants produce lovely flower heads and make good ground cover to prevent the soil from drying out so readily in the summer, so consider placing them around other tall-growing, water-hungry plants in the vegetable garden (such as legumes, cucumbers, or tomatoes) to maximize space and productivity.

They are considered perennial (as with Jerusalem artichoke) because no matter how hard you aim to harvest them all, you will invariably end up leaving some in the ground so they will spring into productivity again the following spring.

Savvy Tip: Do keep a few back from your harvest and store them in soil in a frost-free location to use for replanting next year and help ensure the continued production of these edibles.

Growing preferences: Oca struggles in high temperatures about 85°F (29°C). Provide some partial shade among taller shaded plantings if needed. It also likes a lot of water, so again a mixed planting system with different layers and ground cover will work best.

Horseradish

Packed with flavor, this little-appreciated root deserves a resurgence of interest. It is very easy to grow; you just need to choose your location wisely because once established, it will be nearly impossible to remove. The leaves are edible as well as the roots, and it is a bit of an all-around superfood. It is great during the winter mixed into dishes, adding a flavor punch akin to mustard. It's also incredibly good for you as a preventative, anti-inflammatory hero that can help boost your immune system overall. Horseradish is right up there with garlic in terms of health benefits, so try to add it to meals at each and every opportunity.

I harvest the root later in the year and grate it. I then mix the grated horseradish with vinegar and some salt so it is preserved for continued use over winter. The plants will grow back with gusto for years and help you on your resilient gardening journey. Consider growing horseradish in a gravel garden to help keep it contained.

↓ Jerusalem artichokes will grow tall, so be mindful when choosing where to plant them.

Jerusalem Artichoke

I mentioned the prebiotic nature of this plant and its benefits as a wind break and er, wind producer combined. It's also nice and straightforward to grow. Just choose your spot wisely again because once established, it will have its roots anchored (literally) in that spot and be hard to remove.

Plant Jerusalem artichoke tubers in a sunny spot, about 4 inches (10 cm) below the ground in well-composted soil with about 1 foot (30 cm) between each plant. Choose a location on the outskirts of your plot if you can as you want to keep this tall-growing plant from adversely casting too much shade on other nearby plants. Also, it is useful to provide protection against the elements, so an outside positioning on your vegetable garden tends to work best.

Harvest the tubers later in the year. They benefit from a touch of frost first and then you can eat them fresh, straight after picking as the don't keep very well; that is why you never see them for

VEGETABLE GARDEN PLANTING GUIDE

sale in shops. If you can't keep them in the ground until you want to harvest more, or if you'd like to pick more of them than you can eat quickly, keep the harvested tubers in a box of compost to try to preserve their quality for as long as possible.

Their lush, nutty flavor makes a welcome addition to a range of stews, sliced or diced. I also like them roasted and added to mash, soups, or casseroles where their flavor packs a punch. Do remember, though, that sharing is caring, and any excess wind caused by eating them is because you are feeding your healthy gut microbiome. It's less of an embarrassment if this experience is shared by all!

Savvy Tip: There are generally few issues with an established Jerusalem artichoke patch, but do prevent your beds from becoming too dense with tubers, which can happen if too many are left in the ground from the previous year. This will reduce the size of the crop and crowded beds can enhance the risk of fungal disease and reduce the water absorption and retention ability of soil. Also watch out because these generally very resilient plants can spread far and wide.

The tubers don't keep well once harvested, so it can be useful to cover beds with a fleece or mulch (such as spent foliage) to enable you to better harvest more lovely nutty tubers in the dark depths of winter.

↓ Perennial sea kale growing naturally in the wild

Perennial Kales and Brassicas

There are many different varieties of these long-lasting leafy plants that dutifully keep growing year after year. Also known as cottager or homesteader kales here in the United Kingdom, they are a valuable source of food all year round. And they are super resilient to boot. They seem able to shake off a mild pest attack with no issue at all, due to their deeper-rooted, perennial nature.

Just some of the varieties available include 'Taunton Dean', 'Purple Tree', 'Asturian Tree Cabbage'. There is also sea beet.

Certain birds can be problematic with attacking the seedlings, but once established, your plants will be super hardy. Just pick off caterpillars, keep harvesting the leaves frequently, and apply a mulch to protect from severe drought. Mixed planting also helps deter any issues.

Other Perennials Worth Growing

There are many other perennial crops, including Egyptian walking onions, skirret, wild garlic, three-cornered leek, Good King Henry, Chinese artichoke, and groundnut.

← Skirrets growing in my garden. This is a perennial root that was eaten in Europe before the potato was introduced.

Sorrel

This hardy herb is included here because its leaves are so incredibly versatile in the kitchen. I grow it in my polytunnels and outside, and it dutifully returns year after year. Keep picking it to encourage fresh growth as the baby leaves are best to work with. It seems to stand firm come rain, shine, wind, or storm. Magic.

Globe Artichokes and Cardoon

In warmer climates, globe artichokes can grow on for a number of years, hence their inclusion here in the perennials section. They are rather sensitive to cold and to extreme heat and wet conditions, so I grow cardoon instead. My cardoon grows in an old tractor tire with the spent foliage and thistle heads providing food for birds and a home for insects over winter, before being used to mulch the emerging new growth in spring. Although edible (you can blanch the stems), I prefer to grow cardoon for purely ornamental purposes as their unique tall thistle heads bring a smile to my face.

Globe artichokes are too much work in my growing conditions, so I don't bother anymore. They require a lot of watering and ideally milder overwinter conditions to truly prosper.

If you live in a milder climate and choose to grow artichokes, mulch and compost the plants heavily to reduce watering requirements and consider that weakened plants will become more susceptible to pests. I personally find the process of harvesting and cooking the heads not really worth it for the amount of artichoke heart inside, although the flesh is incredibly good for you, so it's a matter of how much growing it means to you. For me, it's the wrong plant for my place, so the work involved outweighs the benefit of growing.

Yacón

Like oca, yacón produces underground tubers. Also like oca, it is best to harvest those tubers and keep a few back in storage (in a box of moist compost in a cool but frost-free room) to replant the following year. These are well worth the grow. Plant out purchased seed tubers in spring, once the first risk of any frost has passed, into compost-rich, fertile soil. You harvest these delicious pear/potato-like tubers late in the season, but the wait is well worth it.

They are super hardy, pest- and disease-free, and resilient once they get fully established. So mulch them to help them on their way. As well as the delicious tubers, the leaves are also edible as wraps for other foods. The roots have a prebiotic nature and can be made into a type of syrup. So many uses, so little time. If you can grow Jerusalem artichokes, you can grow yacón and you'll never look back.

Resilient Growing Advice for Traditional Crops

In this section, I'll share ways to make traditional garden crops more resilient in the face of a changing climate, offering tips and advice for improved success and bigger harvests.

TOMATOES

These water-hungry plants can really struggle during a heatwave and have been predicted to be one of the crops likely to become challenged in the future in our changing climate. To help ensure continued crop success, choose your tomato varieties wisely and keep experimenting with others. Depending on where you live and what space you have available, choose accordingly. For example, bush varieties of tomatoes are better for pots and containers, while taller, indeterminate varieties need more space and require staking for support. Tomatoes do require a lot of sunshine and a longer growing season in order to ripen, so smaller fruits such as cherry tomatoes might be a better if the conditions are cooler where you live as they grow and ripen quicker than bigger varieties such as beefsteak tomatoes.

The risk of blight can be an issue, particularly in cool or especially hot summers. Also, the risk of a late frost that can decimate seedlings overnight may occur more often where you live. There are lots of protections you can put in place however, and I have grown tomatoes in low-water conditions successfully for years.

Extreme Weather Tomato Growing

I have allowed my tomatoes to grow completely wild in extended periods of drought, training them along the ground and allowing the stems to root wherever they touched the soil, with lots of plants grown between to protect the soil, and they fared fantastically. The mixed planting system I employ means I have lots of space (at least 5 feet [1.5 m] between plants), so it's harder for blight to get a hold and spread. My no-dig, microorganism-rich soil must have come to the tomato plants aid as it's amazing how well they fared. No split tomatoes, bumper harvests for weeks on end, and huge sprawling plants growing far and wide across the beds. It just goes to show what can be done if you exert less control and make the most of a natural growing system's potential to thrive in times of challenge—in this case by emulating the way wild tomatoes grow naturally.

↑ **ABOVE, FROM LEFT**
Here, I'm in my poly-tunnel with tomatoes that have been allowed to spread and root to build greater resilience.

Tomato plant rooting on the stem

VEGETABLE GARDEN PLANTING GUIDE

KIM'S TIP

Savvy Tips for Tomato Resilience

Plant Deeply

Plant seedlings deep into the ground when planting them out. Plant them up to their highest set of two leaves, in fact. This enables the plant to establish much deeper, bigger roots that will give the plant the best chance of success.

Root the Stems

Try rooting some of the stems of your tomato plants. Do so by laying one of them along the ground to encourage roots to form where the stem touches the soil. You can then stake the plant above the further root growth. To aid the process of rooting, cover the stem up with earth at points to anchor it, or even hold it down in place with a few stones. What this means in essence is that with additional roots, your plant is able to source water and nutrients from a much wider area, which in turn provides a greater robustness against drought while also encouraging bumper harvests in return.

Free-Plant and Use Ground Cover

An experience with blight in the polytunnels—where my tomato plants succumbed to this airborne disease within a few short weeks—really got me thinking about the way I plant. This was back when I first moved to my homestead, and I realized that the close proximity of the tomatoes (side by side in a long row) was enabling this pesky disease to easily spread. This is when I started free-planting, just as an experiment to begin with—leaving at least 5 feet (1.5 m) between plants and mixing other crops in-between. It has worked beautifully in so many ways, and it totally nailed the blight risk, hands down.

The surrounding crops can come to the tomato plants' aid during a period of heat as they will protect the soil from drying out. Choose low edible cover crops, such as nasturtium or calendula, particularly around the base of the tomato stems. Although I have tried most crops, salad leaves and herbs also work well, just try to not plant water-hungry crops too close together.

Don't Over-Pamper Your Plants

This is absolutely key, and when planting in a bigger bed—with a healthy robust, compost-rich soil—there is no need at all for added fertilizers. Added feed will make your tomato plants lazy and will stop them forming symbiotic relationships with the beneficial soil life. Too much water will also stop them from forming deeper root systems that they need to help them stand firm during a heatwave. Less really is more.

Tomatoes in pots will require feed more frequently; use mulches to help hold water in pots for longer. When you water, do so deeply and directly into the soil itself for longer periods of time, but less frequently. A mulch can be used on top to help keep moisture in. See page 74 on mulching options.

CARROTS

Carrots are such a vegetable patch staple you wouldn't necessarily know that they have been bred from the original wild carrot to look the way they do (orange and tapered). They were first domesticated in the Afghanistan region before being further bred into the commercial deep orange varieties we know today in the seventeenth century by Dutch horticulturists. In the future, many of the most commonly available varieties may no longer be fit for purpose. Certainly root splitting will become an increasing challenge, as will a greater risk of pest and disease as our climate warms and extreme rain and heat become more of an issue.

These delectable roots struggle with deep changes to watering; too much water can cause the cells to expand and crack. Too little water, and much the same can occur. Clay soils are more of a challenge because it is hard for roots to spread readily.

Improve Soil and Improve Your Carrot Yield

Whatever type of soil you have and whatever carrot varieties you grow, building soil structure is key. Composted and mulched loam is better able to protect the carrots growing within from extreme water-level fluctuations that can cause splitting. It will help retain moisture for longer and improve your soil's ability to support good carrot growth. Leaf mold and wood chips work especially well as a thin mulch over carrot beds.

Choose Your Varieties Well

Soil improvement won't happen overnight, so as you build fertility and microorganism-rich loam, consider using smaller varieties of carrot, rather than deep roots, especially if clay soil is currently a challenge. This also is the case if growing carrots in pots or containers. Go for the mini carrot varieties; they are just as delicious.

Consider trying some of the heritage and more unusual varieties such as purple-, pink-, yellow-, or red-skinned carrots; they may offer attractive flavor and climate change–savvy resilience.

There are trials being conducted that examine the resilience of wilder varieties of carrot by the Crop Wild Relatives Project. Lots of partner gardens, such as Kew Gardens in the United Kingdom, are trailing wild varieties of carrot alongside traditional selections to compare and contrast results.

Savvy Tips

I prefer to sow my carrot seed in seed trays before planting out whole. I love the baby carrot thinnings, which I cook whole with the tops. By sowing five or six seed per module, I can plant out whole to avoid damaging the carrot roots. I put these whole clumps of carrot in and around other gaps in my free-planting system, therefore making it much harder for carrot flies to find my precious roots.

When harvesting carrots on a dry day, squeeze some strong-smelling herb leaves to cover the trail of the scent and take your harvested carrots inside pronto. This will further help prevent carrot fly issues as they are drawn in by the smell of the carrot tops and can sniff it out from very far away.

BEETS

These delectable roots have a lot of natural resilience built in. The varieties that don't bolt good soil will again help your vegetable garden cope with water when it is in ample supply and scarce.

Minimize risk: Pest- and disease-wise, two common threats include the beet leaf miner and Cercospora leaf spot, which tends to spread in wet conditions, causing reddish-ringed spots on beet foliage. In the case of beet leaf miner, parasitic wasps and garden birds can keep numbers in check, so boosting biodiversity and natural pest control will be key. Also, not having large blocks of beets planted together helps prevent spread of both pest and disease.

FRENCH, BROAD, BUSH, AND POLE BEANS

So many exciting varieties to grow, so little time. Planting a diversity of varieties is very helpful in finding the types of beans that work for you in your area. Wet weather can cause issues with fungal disease and aphids can be a problem, especially if plants are weakened through weather stress. Also, there can be issues with flowers not setting pods properly during extreme weather events such as storms and drought. These are the main issues to mitigate with growing beans. Late frost can decimate non-cold-hardy varieties. Wait until risk of frost has passed before planting. I favor sowing the seeds indoors, then transplanting the plants outdoors so the seedlings are as robust as possible when planted out. This helps them stand firm against any early pest issues.

Soil Health Equals Healthier Plants

Well-composted no-dig soil helps boost resilience and hold and maintain water for longer. Mulching can be helpful after planting out and while plants become established, and also to mitigate extreme drought.

Pollination Issues

Really hot, cold, wet, or windy conditions can hinder pollinators from getting to work pollinating your beans. No pollinators equals no harvest. Protecting your plot against extreme weather through layered planting with lots of habitat that's attractive to pollinators will help solve this issue. It creates a more sheltered spot against the elements (see page 53 on using the layering of plants) so that pollinators can still be active for longer. It also welcomes a greater number of potential pollinators to make your garden home. The more insects you have on hand, the greater the opportunity for effective pollination.

Picking beans regularly will help the plant conserve enough energy to keep producing pods. Mixed planting with lots of pollinator-attractive plants will further aid effective bean production.

↑ **ABOVE, FROM TOP**
Beets and carrots being harvested

Different bean varieties

VEGETABLE GARDEN PLANTING GUIDE

The Three Sisters Guild

This complimentary combination of legume, squash, and corn (and amaranth for a four sisters guild) were used by Native Americans more than 3,000 years ago. It is arguably the earliest example of companion planting. In the United Kingdom where I live, the system doesn't work as the climate isn't warm enough to support such a combination, but I do find winter squash with sweet corn works well. I favor planting any legume with a brassica alongside so that the brassica can benefit directly from the nitrogen-fixing properties of the legume. You need to leave the legumes root in the soil after it has finished producing to fully appreciate this gain. Experiment with what works in your zone. Make guilds that work in your own garden.

Savvy Tips: Free-planting systems with plenty of natural pest control keep pest numbers in check. Healthy plants will be less susceptible to attack from aphids and other pests. You can use shading during really hot weather to help plants cope and avoid scorch damage to leaves.

ZUCCHINI/COURGETTE, WINTER SQUASH, AND PUMPKINS

Too much water can result in fungal issues and the proliferation of rot; too little water and your plants will struggle. Although generally easy to grow, extreme weather and pest issues can cause challenges.

→ I harvest a lot of zucchini from my gardens.

Lack of pollination can be a problem. The key things to do are:

- Boost soil health and water deeply, followed by mulch.
- See which varieties others are growing successfully in your area, and try those
- Attract pollinators in with wider, mixed-planted beds. Herbs such as marjoram, thyme, and oregano can be quick pollinator attractors. In the interim, consider also hand pollinating plants (moving pollen from the male flowers to female flowers) using a small paintbrush.

Savvy Tip: If seed saving, tie female flowers closed with string after hand pollinating first thing in the morning, if you're considering saving seeds from this crop and you have other varieties of squash growing nearby.

BRASSICAS

There are so many varieties from which to choose, but it's important to work with those that you enjoy eating. Weigh the pros and cons of growing any types that might struggle in your climate. Not all brassicas are created equal when it comes to natural resilience, and our changing climate presents many challenges. As well as a greater risk of pest and disease (especially with overwintering) and multiple breeding opportunities, stressed plants are more vulnerable to attack. In addition to these, confused plants can bolt (sending up flowers) when you least expect it. During a cold spring or a hot, hot summer, for example, natural survival instincts to reproduce may kick in prematurely. Mixed planting is beneficial, as is choosing varieties that work best in your area and trying not to necessarily fight too hard to rejuvenate those that struggle.

To give you an example of my own experiences, I don't like having to net anything in my gardens to keep pests out, so in my free-planted system, I grow varieties that are low-maintenance and fuss-free. This means I just grow pick-and-come-again leafed brassicas (such as kales), romanesco, kohlrabi and purple sprouting broccoli mainly, with rutabagas/swedes and turnips. No netting and no crop rotation is required, just lots of different plantings and space in between the brassicas all mixed in. From there, I let my ample pest patrol friends work their magic. This doesn't mean I don't have to remove any caterpillars or bugs, I do, but they are kept in better balance overall. It's an eat-and-be-eaten world with plenty of super fuss-free produce for me and my family.

↑ **ABOVE, FROM LEFT**
Romanesco is more resilient than cauliflower.

Kohlrabi is also very hardy and delicious to eat.

THE WINNERS

The perennial kales win hands down on the resilience scales. See the section of perennials on page 170 for more on the different varieties and options available. Otherwise, purple sprouting broccoli can be grown for a few years as it develops nice deep roots. Chard seems to grow on and on, and kohlrabi is a nice hardy option that's able to stand firm rather amply during challenging weather before shooting back into new growth shortly thereafter.

THE MORE CHALLENGING CHOICES

Cauliflower and Brussels sprouts have very exacting watering requirements and that can cause issues in topsy-turvy weather. This doesn't mean they can't be grown, but in a drought scenario they will be more work than other crops. You'll need to keep them sufficiently quenched, week in and week out. Other options include looking at different varieties of cauliflowerlike vegetables and growing these instead. One viable alternative worth considering is romanesco, a cross between cauliflower and broccoli. It has less exacting watering needs.

BALL-HEADED CABBAGES

If you love them, grow them, but they do take up a lot of space and can house pests inside, so personally I don't bother anymore. This is a good example of choosing your leaf according to what works best for you and your space. Don't be afraid to ditch varieties that take too much effort. It's your garden, your decision.

Hero Crops with More Natural Resilience Built In

Here are just some of my favorite all-time resilient vegetable patch heroes. If something sounds interesting, give it a go. It is fun to experiment, and if climate change adaptation is your goal, then turn this into a positive and see if you can make your vegetable gardens more diverse and flavor-laden as a result.

Field beans Although most commonly associated with livestock fodder, these hardy, small growing, overwintered crops are from the same family as broad beans. They are very edible and resilient indeed. Field beans are often grown in countries such as Egypt as an alternative to chickpeas and are well worth a look. They can be grown easily as a winter or spring crop.

Tomatillo Although commonly associated with salsa, this vigorous grower produces fruits that are very versatile in the kitchen. They can be roasted and added to a variety of dishes. They are easier to grow than tomatoes, and they make a nice addition to the resilient vegetable garden. I can even grow them outside in my exposed spot in the United Kingdom where I can't grow tomatoes. Indoors or out, once established they will produce a bumper harvest that is hard to beat.

Cucamelon As the name suggests, this vining edible is a cross between a cucumber and a melon and boy does it spread. The little tasty fruits are great in salad or kids'
packed lunch boxes, and in a greenhouse or polytunnel the plant can grow back the following year.

'Crystal Lemon' Cucumber I've never grown cucumbers as rampant as these before. They are prolific growers. I allow them to trail along the ground and do their thing, growing out from the raised beds and over the gravel, providing me with ample harvests with no effort at all. These lovely round, lemony-flavored cucumbers are also very versatile to eat and store well.

Amaranth This plant is a resilient hero. It is commonly grown in Africa for its spinach-like leaves and its grain (seed), which can be used like quinoa. It has helped my hungry fruits survive with little water during heatwaves as its sprawling tendencies have provided essential ground cover, protecting the soil and plants growing nearby. So many benefits, and it will self-seed with abandon, providing you with free plants for many years to come.

↑ **ABOVE, FROM LEFT** The 'Crystal Lemon' cucumber growing semi-wild in my gardens is super resilient.

Amaranth harvest of edible leaves

10 Plant Protection

Learn how to use structures and plant covers to protect your veggie plants from climate extremes.

AS OUR POOR PLANET FLITS from one extreme to another more frequently, and as seasons as we have known them are becoming unreliable and erratic, some form of protection for plants is key. Following exacting instructions on seed packets also is no longer a given for success as planting times depend on the weather, instinct, and your ability to ensure your seedlings have the temperature they need to flourish.

A warm spell early on in the season can catch many gardeners unawares. With a distinct feeling of spring in the air, the desire to start planting can be strong. Yet, this warm weather could surely be followed by a temperature dip and cold snap that can kill cold-sensitive seedlings if sufficient shelter and warmth isn't provided.

Preparing for any eventuality is important, as is minimizing the amount of work involved for you the gardener. Lugging lots of seedlings back and forth from your house, thanks to an unpredictable climate, is laborious.

In this chapter, we will look at under-cover structures, as well as ways to offer protection using other plants and materials for gardens of every size. It also discusses options for food production all year round as there are many season-extension options for home-grown edibles at your green-thumbed disposal. Saving money, reducing plastic from store-brought vegetables, and overwintering garden produce all have a feel-good factor guaranteed. It's a climate change–savvy gardener must-do during the coldest, darkest months of the year.

← Lovely pick-and-come-again salad leaves you can grow all winter long

↑ Me with some of my indoor edibles

Wonderful Windowsill Edibles Inside Your Home

Growing indoors is a great, fun, and confidence-boosting activity at any time of the year, but arguably it especially comes into its own over winter when outside growing opportunities are somewhat limited. Keep on growing, nurturing, and tending plants all year round, and the darker days of winter won't seem quite so bleak. Plus, you'll have extra delicious edibles at your fingertips.

There are many fun projects for children and big kids alike, and turning leftover materials into new plants is a meaningful and enjoyable activity with oodles of extra brownie points on the resilience front as it shows resourcefulness.

MICROGREENS

Even on the smallest windowsill you can grow a decent supply of these luscious baby leaves. Just choose a sunny sill and a container that fits on it. Fill it with growing media and pack in your seeds of choice. Choose from any brassica seed such as cabbage, kale, chard, mizuna/mibuna, and bok choy. These leaves are great for use in winter salads and as edible decoration for meals to impress.

FOOD STORE SEEDLINGS

Let's face it, many of us have packets of healthy, wholefood ingredients we love the idea of, but they invariably end up ignored (and getting dusty) at the back of a cupboard. I'd wager dried pulses are likely to be among the most commonly bought, but forgotten about, items confined to the dark depths of your food store. Fret not; they are among some of the best ingredients for indoor growing opportunities over winter. Here's how.

Pea Shoots

These delectable shoots are so delicious in salads or used to decorate food. They are dead easy to grow on a windowsill. Just take some of your peas, soak them in water overnight, and then plant in some seed-starting mix on a windowsill. Again, a shallow planting tray is just fine here as it's small plants we are growing for multiple pickings. As you harvest, leave some new growth on each plant to grow again for more harvesting opportunities.

Micro Herbs

Again, this is a great way to use leftover out-of-date herb seeds. Sow fennel, cilantro/coriander, cumin, dill, mustard, and fenugreek seed into windowsill pots and cover with plastic or glass to help raise the temperature until they germinate. You can have a veritable mini garden of herby happiness at your fingertips in even the smallest space.

Salad Sprouts

You can buy chickpea, alfalfa, mung bean, and lentil sprouts from most health food stores and they are delicious eaten raw in salad or stir fried, with a lovely nutty flavor and crunchy texture. Growing some at home is very straightforward. You can either buy a sprouting tray or make your own from a large screw-top jar and lid. Make holes in the lid and add your sprouting seeds of choice, soaking it in water overnight and turning the jar upside down to drain out the remaining liquid before rinsing again, draining, and then leaving the jar upside down in a warm, sunny spot to germinate. After a few days—and with a daily rinse of water—the shoots will start to emerge. When they do, it's time to wash your sprouts and place them in the fridge for use within a couple of days. Delicious.

← Grow pea shoots indoors over winter.

PLANT PROTECTION

SALAD LEAVES

Pick-and-come-again salad leaves are easiest to grow indoors as they afford more opportunity for multiple pickings. You can buy mixed variety packs or work with a single variety like 'Salad Bowl'. As with the microgreens and herbs, plant more thickly because the plants won't grow to full size and therefore don't need as much space. You can keep on picking all winter long. For more indoor growing ideas and inspiration see page 184.

Savvy Structures and Covers for the Vegetable Garden

Being prepared for topsy-turvy weather is incredibly important and having a range of materials at your disposal for doing so really helps. Once purchased, these items can be stored away and used again and again for many seasons and years to come. Vegetable garden covers can help you further continue your growing later in the year, protect seedlings against frost, and offer shade for plants in a heatwave.

→ Mixed planting also helps afford protection against weather extremes, pests, and disease.

HOOPS AND FRAMES

There are many readily available structures, so choose those that best work around your existing growing beds. If they are not permanently attached, the covers can easily be put in place when required. Just ensure your structure is firmly secured to avoid storm damage or loss.

Portable under-cover structures can be moved from place to place as needed. Plastic or enviro-mesh covers can help raise the temperature early and late in the year and also help with late frost protection for sensitive plants. Or if it's a cold spring, they can be used to encourage earlier harvests.

As well as bought frames, you can have some thrifty fun my making your own out of wood such as willow or hazel, an old trampoline frame, or whatever materials can be easily salvaged. One person's junk is another's makeshift cloche.

Covers

Covers come in many different materials, shapes, and sizes, and they can be draped over plants/raised beds or attached to a frame of some form. From insect-proof netting to help fend off cabbage butterfly, to plastic sheeting for temperature raising, to row cover fleece to protect against cold, to shade covers to help with extreme heat—there's a cover at the ready for whatever the weather.

Cold Frame

Cold frames are useful for protecting plants against cold early and late in the year. I favor moveable cold frames using windows and old shower doors on top of raised beds (see page 94).

Cloches

There are many brands and shapes and sizes on the market to buy, or you can improvise with propagator lids, plastic bottles cut in half, and all sorts of leftover tubs and trays. They all do the job perfectly well to safely enclose plants and raise the temperature when needed.

↑ **ABOVE, FROM TOP**
Vegetable garden hoop and netting structure

Here I am applying a cover in my polytunnel early in the year to warm the soil for planting.

PLANT PROTECTION

↑ **CLOCKWISE, FROM TOP LEFT** One of my polytunnels with a light dusting of snow

Ventilation is also key in an under-cover structure.

I love planting in my polytunnel for winter.

Greenhouse and Polytunnel Growing

If you want to take your year-round growing to the next level, it's worth considering a bigger, permanent polytunnel or greenhouse as a long-term addition to your outside space. There are rules and regulations around such structures, which will vary depending on where you live, whether it's a listed building, an allotment and how close you are to neighbors, any roads nearby, and so on and so forth. Normally though, it's perfectly permissible to add something in, as long as it's smaller and considered for domestic, rather than commercial, use.

If you know someone in your area with a polytunnel, then why not go have a chat with them to see if they came up against any issues just to be on the safe side, especially if you have neighbors that might be likely to complain. Generally speaking though, as long as it's small and doesn't cause any issues with neighbors or access, then you should be fine.

Thrifty Under-Cover Option

It is possible to source old greenhouses and polytunnels for free. Your local Freecycle chapter or homestead group might provide notification of any that become available in your area. Also, if you see a structure that is unused, then why not ask its owner directly? Often people will be grateful for the opportunity to clear out an unused structure if you are happy to organize its safe removal and reconstruction your end. I have dug out a polytunnel structure myself by hand and it is perfectly possible to do; it's just easier with a few people lending a helping hand.

Where to Site Any Structure

North-to-south always used to be the recommended orientation to maximize the amount of available sunlight for the produce growing inside. Now though, with climate change, you might want to reconsider. During a period of prolonged heat, such structures can get too hot too quickly, causing serious issues for the plants growing inside. West-to-east can help, but trees or hedging nearby are worth a consideration. They help cast some daytime shade and can help slow the flow of strong wind, further protecting your precious under-cover space.

How to Decide Which Structure Is Best for You

The options can be rather daunting and more than a little overwhelming. It helps to see what others have done to get ideas of how it might look in your own outside space. Polytunnels are cheaper than greenhouses to buy and you tend to get more for your money, so a lot of people opt for these if they are looking for a larger, more expansive structure.

Greenhouses arguably look more attractive and are longer lasting in terms of the structure and covering. You can, however, generally pack more into a polytunnel and it's the plastic cover that requires replacement every four of five years (as recommended), yet they can last a lot longer in principle if you look after them. I have a poly-tunnel with a cover that is now fifteen years old and still working productively.

KEY UNDER-COVER TIPS

Ensure that you have sufficient ventilation for crops growing under cover. It's also inte-gral in a resilient growing system to try to allow the natural world in as much as you can. It's essential that pollinators have access to your plants, and you want to create as much biodiversity as you can inside of your growing structure for natural pest control pur-poses. This simply won't work if your space is cut off from the outside world with netting or screens. See page 151 on natural pest control for information here on the importance of predators for natural pest control.

Ventilation

Even during the cold, dark winter months, it's important to air your under-cover space if it is actively growing crops. Doing so helps to prevent a buildup of airborne fungal spores, which can otherwise proliferate over winter in dark, damp, cold conditions. Try to create airflow at least once a week, ideally on the most clement of days—even if only for an hour or so.

During summer, or in a heatwave, leave doors and windows open overnight as much as you can to help create a cooler start to the day. In intense sunshine an under-cover space can heat incredibly quickly, challenging the plants within.

Watering

Even more so than outside, it's important to water the ground and not the leaves of the crops growing in a greenhouse or polytunnel. This helps reduce blight risk and maximizes water absorption during the summer, and it helps prevent mold over winter. Water early in the day or later in the evening. See page 70 for more wise watering tips.

Repair and Secure Structures

Any polytunnel tears or loose fixtures can quickly become an issue in a storm. Remember to batten down the hatches and secure structures as much as you can. Tape any holes to maximize the longevity of your under-cover growing spaces.

What Can You Grow Under Cover?

You can extend the growing season on either end, meaning that harvests can arrive earlier and later in the year. And you can grow all year round on a larger scale. Many people don't make use of their under-cover spaces at all over winter. Try it! A lot can be reliably grown with such protection from the worst of the winter extremes.

Baby carrots and beets, salad leaves, fennel, and cilantro/coriander, as well as winter and Asian greens, can be grown all winter long. Seeds can be germinated a bit earlier with extra space for seedling protection, and you can try more exotic crops.

I live more than 700 feet (213 m) above sea level in the Wild West of Wales, and I simply can't grow tomatoes or peppers outside, so polytunnels are essential for me to grow a much wider variety of Mediterranean crops.

Raising the Temperature

During the cold months of the year when you are keen to carry on growing, here are some ideas to help:

- Create a cold frame inside of your polytunnel (a layer within a layer). This is great for protecting seedlings should the temperature really plummet.

- Try solar heating kits. Solar is becoming more reliable and cost effective.

- A hot bed can be created in a barrel or box that can create heat and act as a propagator for seedlings. A hot bed is made by adding rotting horse manure to a barrel or box and placing potted seedlings on top of it. The idea is that the heat released from the decomposition of the manure can raise the temperature inside of the bed.

- I find layered planting helps afford protection really well, even in my polytunnel. For example, my overwintered brassica plants help to protect the cilantro/coriander and lettuce growing next to it.

Under-Cover Resilient Inspiration: Seed Saving

Having some form of protection enables you to widen the amount of seed that can be reliably home-save. This is because no matter the weather outside, you can help ensure protection for plants as they flower and set seed to avoid plants such as lettuce from going moldy in a wet summer. Further you can provide protection to help prevent plants crossing, which some of the outbreeder crops (such as brassicas and carrots) can otherwise do. See page 111 for more information on seed-saving success.

Enjoy Your Space

I think it's absolutely essential to have some form of seating in an under-cover space—even a folding chair so you can sit and truly enjoy the fruits of your labor all year round, whatever the weather. I even have a little stove in mine that I can use with the doors open. I have been known to have a little snooze at times in the comfy chairs; it's simply so relaxing.

11 Troubleshooting Guide

Helpful solutions to some of climate change's biggest vegetable gardening challenges, including timesaving tips.

Can't buy your own peat-free growing medium? Here's how to make your own.

There are huge issues with the use of peat in horticulture. While the United Kingdom is banning its use and therefore has an increasing number of peat-free growing mediums now available to buy, many countries do not offer the same choice and alternative opportunities.

You can make and source some of your own peat-free ingredients to save money and further enhance resilient composting supplies. Here's how:

There is a plethora of advice on home compost making on page 73. To boost the supply you make, consider adding extra supercharged ingredients available locally to you, such as seaweed, nettle leaves, comfrey, borage, chicken or poultry bedding, manure, and sheep wool.

Homemade growing mixes are also possible with the use of rotted leaves or wood chips. See page 93 for more information on this and how to make your own mulches and homegrown soil improvers for free.

← Make your own compost. Here I am with my compost bin made from salvaged materials.

Having issues with peat-free mixes?

If you are experiencing quality control issues with purchased peat-free growing mediums, try mixing it in with your own supply or using thinner layers on beds. For seedlings, be mindful that sometimes peat-free ingredients, such as coir, can make soil look dry on top, but it can be too moist underneath. Putting your finger in to check is the surefire solution to regulate correct water use.

Over time you will be able to adjust and find the right brand/homemade combination that works for you. Just remember you are helping to keep carbon in the ground by going peat-free.

I can't afford to buy much this year for gardening. What should I do?

Don't worry; gardening doesn't have to be expensive. There are lots of materials that can be sourced for free and opportunities to garden in a low-cost way. Know also that spending less is good for the planet and can help build further resilience skills in the process as a low-cost approach isn't just financial; it is extremely climate change–savvy to boot.

↑ **ABOVE, FROM LEFT** Get working on making your own compost now so you won't have any issues with availability.

Save your own seed, share tools, and barter and exchange to save money. It's fun and free.

Reach out to local gardening clubs, groups, and associations online and in person in your area. Seed swaps normally occur early in the year and are a fantastic way of securing locally adapted seed for free or just a small entrance fee. Make your own planting pots out of supermarket trays, pots, and packages, and many salvaged materials can be transformed into fantastic upcycled container gardens. Get into your local freecycle group and embrace bartering, swaps, and exchanges locally. Making your own compost will save money longer term, as will seed saving. And you can boost plant supplies with the taking of cuttings.

Know that you will be channeling an older form of gardening, before it all became so commercialized, and doing so will change the way you garden for the better. This is not a lesser approach. My gardening-for-free adventures have empowered me and enriched my growing efforts forever.

I'm going away on vacation for a week and there is a heatwave. How do I keep plants alive?

Don't worry, there are things you can do before you go to help afford sufficient protection for crops in the ground and in pots so you can enjoy your vacation without worrying. Breaks are important.

In the case of plants in the ground, water them deeply into the ground directly around plants, and do so for longer so the water can permeate deeper down. A surface watering is just that and it won't last as long. Now apply a mulch (a few inches or centimeters of grass clippings, compost, wood chips, leaf mold, or even plant foliage) around especially water-hungry plants to help keep moisture in.

If you have bare patches of soil consider covering these with material or mulch (e.g., cardboard) to afford some protection.

Some shading can be useful in cases of extreme heat to provide some shelter to plants. Do be mindful to remove any potential fire hazards near your home if risk of wildfires is an issue and (e.g., water your compost heap).

In the case of pots, similar measures can be applied, but the soil within will dry out more quickly because there is less of it. Some shading will be key. If you can, consider moving pots to a cooler spot for the time you are away.

There is a late frost forecast—how do I protect seedlings?

This can catch a lot of gardeners by surprise early in the year. Topsy-turvy weather means that an early warm spell can get us all excited and sowing for the growing season ahead. Yet, frosts can come late in spring. If you feel compelled to sow seeds early, it is essential that you have a contingency plan in place should the thermostat truly plummet.

Protection against the cold is a key consideration for any frost-sensitive sowings. Succession sowing can help throughout the spring to ensure you maximize the success of seedlings being grown. Cold frames and protective covers are useful and can be fashioned out of waste materials such as old windows or shower curtains, plastic bottle–turned cloches, and many more innovations.

Some of the crops I like growing struggled last year, so do I try them again or go with something different?

There are lots of resilience-building tips in this book that will help save time, money, and shore up the defenses. If you absolutely love a particular variety of crop, try to keep growing it with these extra measures in place and try another variety or two alongside. Some of the familiar plant types we grow today may not work in the future. Climate change is a fast-moving beast, so local experimentation is a must. Provide protection naturally and try out new crops. Then decide for yourself what is possible for the future and if a crop is worth the effort, or if something else is easier and could act as a replacement.

Biodiversity of planting is very important. Try saving seed from the best examples of crops, and source seed from local seed swaps to try to find more adapted specimens to your neck of the woods. This will all help, and it's fun to see what is out there. It may turn out to be even better than what you grow now.

My cabbage beds have been decimated by cabbage white butterfly (cabbage worm). What do I do?

Such a bad infestation requires quick action, so pick off pesky caterpillars and remove damaged leaves. Do look underneath leaves as caterpillars can hide here and look out for eggs because these need to be removed, too. Then give your plants a good long water and mulch with some garden compost if you have it. Place a net or row cover over the top of plants as they likely have been weakened and will now be even more vulnerable to attack.

Consider mixed planting in future for this and all pest threats, to spread out distance between plants of the same kind. This will make it harder for pests to find what they are looking for. Also consider growing perennial kales as they have a greater ability to deal with any attack as their longer-lasting nature and deeper root structure makes them more resilient.

How do I help protect wildlife over winter?

To keep these gardener's little helpers there where you need them for the following growing season, it's important to enable a viable and attractive place for them to overwinter. This is easy to do as long as you don't meticulously tidy your outside space.

Bedding down your garden and vegetable patch in later autumn is actually the worst thing you can

← **FROM FAR LEFT** Water well and use ground cover and mulching to keep plants quenched during a heat wave.

A mulch of wood chips and leaves helps limit soil evaporation.

Seedlings protected in a cold frame

Biodiversity of planting is key for building resilience. Start free-planting and see what works for your plot and you.

↑ **ABOVE, FROM LEFT** Dead wood can provide winter shelter for wildlife such as solitary bees.

It's much harder for the likes of cabbage white butterfly to find its host plant in a mixed planting bed.

Harvest water as much as possible, even from a shed roof.

do in face of increasing extremes of weather. Turning over the soil, cutting back plants, and removing leaves strips your garden bare of much natural resilience against strong winds and winter rain, as well as reducing habitats for wildlife. Removing spent plants and seed heads further compromises the structure of the soil, as well as reducing opportunities for birds to feed and insects to overwinter.

Cutting back dead branches and pruning can remove habitats for beneficial creatures, such as solitary bees, who like to use dead wood and hollow stems in which to sleep out the winter months. Leaf litter removal and extreme tidying also makes it harder for creatures such as frogs, toads, and newts to find somewhere to sleep the cold months away.

Turning over the compost pile in winter is a no-no as it is used by many creatures as a viable protective habitat. The only time I would turn it over is if rats were to become an issue, and even then I would do so carefully to try to avoid disturbing any other inhabitants.

Do also leave out water for birds and additional feed to help them when food in the wild is otherwise scarce.

There is a restriction on water use and a heatwave. How do I keep my plants alive?

Use up any rainwater you have collected and empty barrels or cisterns by watering plants so when rain comes, you can replenish supplies.

Otherwise, water well (deeply and mulch) using a watering can and afford plants shelter where necessary with shade netting. Use gray water from the home (e.g., water from cooking and showers), but first ensure there aren't any toxic or synthetic soaps or other materials in it.

Try to reduce the amount of water your plants need in the future by watering them less to build resilience. If you grow in pots, try to use bigger containers for especially water-hungry plants. Materials such as wool can be used as plant liners to help keep water in.

What do I do to protect my vegetable garden over winter?

Risk of soil erosion is a serious issue over the colder months of the year. Recently turned over and bare soils are the most vulnerable to hard-earned fertility being washed and eroded away. This idea of bedding down the vegetable garden for winter, removing plants that have finished producing, and digging over the soil is the worst thing you can do: You will be releasing carbon into the atmosphere in the process of digging. Your soil will become vulnerable to the weather. And you will be damaging the soil, the microorganisms living within, and the soil's ability to hold and maintain water. Nobody gains in that scenario, not least of all your back from all the needless clearing and digging.

Instead, leave crops in the ground as much as you can, some produce can overwinter and provide early season edibles. See page 181 for more information on this. Plant foliage and seed heads are useful for biodiversity and natural predators, and it will help protect soil. Grow green manures to help maintain soil structure, or use mulches to boost soil life below. Even allow a few noninvasive weeds to grow, to afford better protection against the elements.

I live in such a dry area. How do I collect more rainwater?

I'm afraid water shortages are going to be (and in some regions, already are) an issue and this is only going to increase as our planet warms. There isn't going to be enough water to go around. The use of rainwater and making the best use of what we have to make it go further are going to be crucial strategies moving forwards.

Do try to upscale the amount of rainwater harvesting you do. Even old, cleaned out bins or tanks can be utilized to maximize collection ability. If you have the space and resources, underground water storage tanks also can be employed. Small ponds can be created, which are good for wildlife and for the garden come summer when other water sources have become scarce. Just remember to keep lids on water barrels to reduce condensation and keep leaves and other items from falling in and clogging taps. Ultimately every available roof, shed, greenhouse, poly-tunnel can be utilized for the collection of this precious resource when it is in ample supply.

There are crop shortages in the groceries again this spring. What can I grow quickly to help put food on the table?

Unfortunately, as our weather becomes more volatile, mono-crop planting systems, based as they are around a relatively narrow field of varieties, are going to become vulnerable. They already are, and we've seen rising food costs and shortages of certain goods as harvest reliability is slowly but surely diminished. Regenerative farming offers solutions, and there are solutions to be found from looking to wild crop relatives and wider varieties of seed stock commercially speaking.

On the ground, however, for us consumers and gardeners, growing as much food as you can is an increasingly sensible option. In the colder months of the year, consider growing windowsill edibles and creating cold frames to protect produce growing outside. Leaving crops in the ground the previous winter such as beets and brassica leaves will help provide a spring supply. Quick-growing edibles for under-cover growing include lettuce, arugula/rocket, herbs, micro-greens, radish, and pea shoots.

Climate change feels so overwhelming. I don't think I have the energy to garden this year.

Know that gardening is the medicine, the balm, a truly positive solution in the face of climate change. And growing some food even on a small scale will make you feel really, really good. It will take your mind off all the horrible things happening in the world and enable you to be part of the solution and take some control and well-being back, seed by seed, plant by plant.

Cut yourself some slack by knowing it's harder nowadays for anyone to feel completely okay all the time. We've all been through so much.

↓ No matter how overwhelmed you feel, gardening can help. Something as simple as sniffing a black currant bud in winter to release the smell of black currants is guaranteed to make you feel a little better.

Play with compost—it encourages the release of happy hormone, serotonin into your brain. Plant seeds and watch them grow, and know that there is hope for us all by working with the natural world in the production of food. You will be feeding your soul as much as anything else. Try to switch off from devices and take time to just be in your vegetable garden space. Walk around, look, listen, and tune in and ideas, opportunity, and reinvigoration for life, for vegetable growing, for our planet, can flow on in.

I don't have a lot of time to garden—it all feels like a lot of work generation, I just feel guilty all the time that I'm not doing enough.

Guilt appears to be commonplace across gardeners. I come across this time and time again where highly experienced and beginner gardeners alike are beating themselves up (figuratively speaking) that their vegetable growing space doesn't look like the vegetable gardens they see on TV shows. What they don't see is the team of gardeners behind the scenes, tending it on the presenter's behalf.

The worker cottage gardens of old were much more free-spirited and super low-maintenance putting food on the table without a lot of time and effort involved. Mixed, sprawling planting can better fend for itself, perennials also, while biodiversity creates natural pest control and noninvasive weeds are allowed in to attract predators and potentially provide another edible food source.

I am busy running courses and writing books and newspaper articles so really don't have a lot of time to garden. When I do so, I want it to be enjoyable so I have pushed the boundaries of how much natural systems can lend a helping hand. Less control equals more low-cost, low-maintenance produce—and a greater degree of climate change–savvy resilience overall. It involves a leap of faith to let go of preconceived ideas of gardening and work generation involved, but the more you do, the more your gardening will take on whole new levels of meaning and resilient muscle.

After an extreme weather event, some of my plants look dead. What should I do?
While there is a lot of advice throughout this book on plant and garden protection, you are going to see some plant damage. A storm or drought can cause immediate and longer-term weakness and challenge you might not see issues until the following year (e.g., with perennials).

Either which way, it is always important to allow plants the chance to recover from extreme weather events and not to instantly dismiss them out of hand. You'll be surprised how many plants can bounce back despite outward appearances not looking good. To give a personal example of this, last year's heatwave and lack of water supply severely impacted on my longer-lasting purple sprouting broccoli plants. They showed signs of rotting over winter as a result of summer damage. Rather than panic I left them in place to see what would happen, and low and behold come spring new shoots started appearing from the bottom of the stem, so I simply cut the stem back to conserve the plant energy to grow on, which it did with gusto, further producing a lovely harvest despite the previous damage.

It is always best to wait and look. Don't immediately remove foliage, and certainly not over winter as this can in itself provide protection for the plant until the extreme weather coast is looking a little clearer. Then cut back and allow the plant the opportunity to conserve energy to continue. Do give plants a chance and don't write them off straight away.

Conclusion: How to Connect with and Enjoy Your Vegetable Garden in a Changing Climate.

YOUR CLIMATE CHANGE–RESILIENT VEGETABLE GARDEN is so much more than just a place where you grow food. It is a nurturing haven where you can grow yourself as much as anything. It's a place where you can help reverse nature's decline, do your bit to carbon capture, reduce plastic, and feel that you are part of the solution, part of a bigger shift toward helping to save our planet and ourselves in the process.

It all counts, bee by bee, plant by plant. Nothing beats homegrown fruit and vegetables—picking fresh from plot to table, bursting with flavor, goodness, and natural vitality. You are feeding your soul as much as your stomach.

Yet in this increasingly troublesome world of ours, it is harder to be in a state of calm and well-being for long. There are so many horrible things happening in the world and so many demands on us. It can be hard to switch off and simply be. Increased anxiety (due to climate change and otherwise), increased social media apps, and to-do lists shouting at us . . .

It is incredibly important when you can, as much as you can, at each and every opportunity, to switch off and tune in to your garden. Let nature sooth, amaze, and inspire you.

We need the natural world as much as it needs us. Being in tune with your outside space and with yourself will make you a better gardener. Remember, you are tapping into your prefrontal cortex by being in a state of emotional regulation and that is essential for thinking clearly and problem solving.

↓ Hands holding soil and a seedling about to be planted out offering hope with the backdrop of a summer vegetable garden

← **FROM LEFT** We are all in this together—for person, plate, and planet.

Watch, look, and learn from the mesmerizing natural world.

This is the balm. Soak it in. Let your inner climate change–resilient gardener flow free. It'll change the way you garden forever for the better. Build resilience in your outside space and in you as a person, with hope for a better future for us all. For person, plate, and planet.

We are all in this together.

Happy climate change–savvy gardening.

—Kim

KIM'S TIP

Tune Out to Tune In to Your Garden

- **Leave your gadgets inside** or to one side.
- **Throw your to-do list to the floor.** This is your time, on your terms.
- **Pick some vegetables,** and play with compost. Remember the happy hormone-inducing properties are in there. Walk around.

- **Maybe watch a bed** and see what creatures are there. What are they doing? Watch birds fluttering back and forth, bees pollinating plants. . . . Let nature draw you in.
- **Most importantly, look, listen,** touch by hand, and learn.
- **This is your calm, happy space.** Make it your own.
- **You and the natural world** work together.

Resources

Radjabzadeh, Djawad, et al. "Gut Microbiome-wide Association Study of Depressive Symptoms." *Nature Communications* 13, no. 1 (2022): 7128.

Dowding, Charles, and Stephanie Hafferty. *No Dig Organic Home & Garden: Grow, Cook, Use & Store Your Harvest*. Permanent Publications, 2017.

Fluet-Chouinard, Etienne, et al. "Extensive Global Wetland Loss over the Past Three Centuries." *Nature* 614, no. 7947 (2023): 281–86.

Fowler, Alys. *The Thrifty Gardener: How to Create a Stylish Garden for Next to Nothing*. Octopus, 2018.

Jabbour, Niki. *Growing Under Cover: Techniques for a More Productive, Weather-Resistant, Pest-Free Vegetable Garden*. Storey Publishing, 2020.

Lamp'l, Joe. *The Vegetable Gardening Book: Your Complete Guide to Growing an Edible Organic Garden from Seed to Harvest*. Cool Springs Press, 2022.

Langer, Richard. *The After-Dinner Gardening Book*. Ten Speed Press, 1992.

Lovelock, James. *The Revenge of Gaia: Earth's Climate Crisis & The Fate of Humanity*. Basic Books, 2007.

Lowry, Christopher, et al. "Identification of an Immune-responsive Mesolimbocortical Serotonergic System: Potential Role in Regulation of Emotional Behavior." *Neuroscience* 146, no. 2 (2007): 756–72.

Montgomery, David, et al. "Soil Health and Nutrient Density: Preliminary Comparison of Regenerative and Conventional Farming." PeerJ 10 (2022): e12848.

Morgan, Sally, and Kim Stoddart. *The Climate Change Garden, UPDATED EDITION*. Cool Springs Press, 2023.

NOAA National Centers for Environmental Information (NCEI). U.S. Billion-Dollar Weather and Climate Disasters (2023). https://www.ncei.noaa.gov/access/billions.

Seymour, John. *The New Complete Book of Self-Sufficiency: The Classic Guide for Realists and Dreamers*. Dorling Kindersley Ltd., 2019.

Sheldrake, Merlin. *Entangled life: How Fungi Make Our Worlds, Change Our Minds & Shape Our Futures*. Random House Trade Paperbacks, 2021.

Stickland, Sue. *Back Garden Seed Saving: Keeping Our Vegetable Heritage Alive*. Eco-Logic Books, 2008.

Walliser, Jessica. *Attracting Beneficial Bugs to Your Garden*. Revised and updated second edition. Cool Springs Press, 2022.

Acknowledgments

THANK YOU TO EVERYONE who has supported me in my climate change vegetable garden adventuring over the years, from magazine and newspaper editors to friends, industry allies, family, and many others besides. A special thanks to Jane Perrone, the former gardening editor of *The Guardian*, who in 2013 allowed me to experiment with gardening for free for a number of years for her pages. This experience of extreme no-cost vegetable growing showed what was truly possible. I had to throw away the traditional rule book entirely to experiment with different ways of doing things. It was challenging, empowering, and ultimately completely transformative and has informed my writing and gardening ever since.

This is the book I have been longing to write for many years where I return to these deeper, plucky, and hugely resilient can-do roots.

Winning the Garden Media Guild Beth Chatto award for environmental journalist of the year in 2022 for a later *Guardian* article about my climate change gardening in the high hills of Wales in the UK has also been a huge privilege and honor. I work in such a fantastic supportive industry. Thanks also to Lucy Hall, the former editor of *BBC Gardeners' World* magazine, for support and generous column inches, Laura Hiller from *Grow Your Own* magazine for giving me so much freedom to play, and Garden Organic for choosing me to edit their magazine for so many years. To Sally Morgan, my excellent co-author on *The Climate Change Garden*, and the fantastic team at Cool Springs Press and Quarto. To Savvy Gardening supremo and commissioning editor, Jessica Walliser, for giving me this opportunity; to Steve Roth, Elizabeth Weeks, and Liz Somers; to my rockstar copyeditor, Jenna; and to everyone else working diligently behind the scenes. Thank you also to the hugely inspiring Niki Jabbour for support and green-door openings.

All the attendees on my courses, webinars, and talks over the years deserve a special mention as you are all fabulous and remind me constantly why I love my work and help make it all so incredibly worthwhile and enjoyable. Post-pandemic I have seen the on-the-ground positive impact more so than ever and a special place in my heart remains for all the gardeners I have met that have been struggling with life in some way. Be it sensory overload, depression, heartbreak or stress, the natural world holds so many nurturing benefits, plant by plant, seed by seed, it all makes a difference and offers hope for the future, no matter the weather.

Resilient gardening is as much about the gardener as it is the actual garden and my own experiences of personal adversity in recent years have ultimately helped shape who I am today and what I have to say. They have made me so much stronger and better able to inform, help, and connect. So please know that others' at-times incredibly unkind, insensitive, or coercive controlling behaviors can teach us longer-term to dig deep and blossom in truly beautiful ways.

Little everyday acts of love, understanding, and kindness also go an incredibly long way and are part of the solution in the continued challenging times we are living through.

Lastly, my thanks go to my incredibly supportive and all-round awesome partner John and to my two most amazing boys, Alberto and Arthur. I am so proud, always.

About the Author

KIM STODDART is an award-winning journalist, author, trainer, speaker, garden designer, and all-round champion of climate change–resilient gardening. She has been writing for publications such as *The Guardian* about resilient and low-cost (free) vegetable growing since 2013 and has been contributing to a varied range of publications ever since. From *BBC Gardeners' World* magazine, the *Daily Express*, and *The Telegraph* national newspaper articles, to *The Lancet* medical journal, columns in *Grow Your Own* and *The Country Smallholder* magazines, and a long-term editorship of *The Organic Way* magazine, Kim is well known for her savvy and upbeat solution-focused approach.

In 2022 Kim won the Garden Media Guild environmental journalist of the year award and was a finalist for journalist of the year.

Kim teaches resilient vegetable growing from her climate change training gardens in West Wales in the UK and for many others, including the Royal Horticultural Society, Kate Humble's farm, Garden Organic, the National Botanic Gardens of Wales, the Great Grow Along, and the Northwest Flower & Garden Show. Kim educates gardening groups, local education authorities, social housing providers, and many other organizations focusing on food-growing skills, wellbeing, confidence-building, and overall resilience.

Kim is also a regular media commentator, having appeared on many shows, podcasts, and programs around the world, including *BBC Radio 4*.

With a background in business and social enterprise, Kim has been heavily involved with a range of organizations over the years, helping secure and set up funded community gardens and projects. She feels passionately about the importance of helping make low-cost vegetable growing more accessible for all, further designing climate change–resilient, low-maintenance spaces and helping transform towns and cities into more biodiverse, resilient areas.

Kim is also the co-author of the well-regarded *The Climate Change Garden*.

Index